155.412   83-1931
H885r   Humphrey.
        Reducing stress in children
         through creative relaxation.

The Library
Saint Francis College
Fort Wayne, Indiana 46808

WITHDRAWN

REDUCING STRESS IN CHILDREN THROUGH CREATIVE RELAXATION

REDUCING STRESS IN CHILDREN THROUGH CREATIVE RELAXATION

By

JAMES H. HUMPHREY

*Professor, Division of Human and Community Resources
University of Maryland
College Park, Maryland*

and

JOY N. HUMPHREY

*Education and Lifestyle Change Consultant
Control Data Corporation
Washington, D. C.*

With a Foreword by
Hans Selye, C.C., M.D., Ph.D., D.Sc.
President, International Institute of Stress

CHARLES C THOMAS • PUBLISHER
Springfield • Illinois • U.S.A.

Published and Distributed Throughout the World by
CHARLES C THOMAS • PUBLISHER
2600 South First Street
Springfield, Illinois, 62717, U.S.A.

This book is protected by copyright. No part of it
may be reproduced in any manner without written
permission from the publisher.

© *1981 by* CHARLES C THOMAS • PUBLISHER
ISBN 0-398-04567-4
Library of Congress Catalog Card Number: 81-9017

*With THOMAS BOOKS careful attention is given to all details of
manufacturing and design. It is the Publisher's desire to present books that are
satisfactory as to their physical qualities and artistic possibilities and
appropriate for their particular use. THOMAS BOOKS will be true to those
laws of quality that assure a good name and good will.*

Printed in the United States of America
I-RX-1

Library of Congress Cataloging in Publication Data

Humphrey, James Harry, 1911-
   Reducing stress in children through creative relaxation.

   Includes index.
   1. Stress (Psychology) in children — Prevention.
2. Relaxation — Study and teaching. I. Humphrey, Joy N.
II. Title. III. Title: Creative relaxation.
BF723.S75H85   155.4'12   81-9017
ISBN 0-398-04567-4   AACR2

FOREWORD

THE Humphreys' book, *Reducing Stress in Children Through Creative Relaxation,* is a detailed description of relaxation used as a prophylactic measure, especially against the stress of modern life.

Among the emotional disturbances induced by stress, the most common appear to be aggressiveness, a sense of frustration, and fear, particularly loose anxiety, a condition in which the individual is afraid without knowing precisely of what.

As the child matures, frustration appears as a consequence of stress, mainly due to a loss of goal orientation and the feeling that nothing is worthwhile, which may gradually progress to severe depression. Aggressiveness may result in the development of special hates (especially among different racial, religious, or political groups) or in general irritability and intolerance.

The authors have based their discussion on various forms of relaxation, referring to such well-known relaxation techniques as Edmund Jacobson's thesis of anxiety-relaxation and Herbert Benson's "relaxation response." Other antistress measures such as physical exercise are also explored.

The book contains specific outlines to achieve progressive relaxation procedures creatively geared toward the child. Imagery and creative movement are among the techniques that the authors apply as aids for general and specific relaxation.

The authors' concern is clearly to orient these ideas of creative movement to result in guidelines that can serve in the positive emotional development of the child.

The analysis of the process of creative movement is particularly noteworthy as this is an area of study that has rarely been explored in current stress research. The approaches to movement, identified by the authors as individual interpretation (improvisation) and dramatization, are presented in a clear, factual manner and described in a language easily acceptable to an instructor or therapist.

The learning code set by the authors to provide important guidelines for the learning experience of the child is reminiscent of our own concept, wherein it is given that man needs stress and that it is desirable for him to use his faculties to the maximum of their tolerance for eustress. In everyday life we must distinguish between two types of stress effects, namely, eustress and distress. Depending upon conditions, stress is associated with desirable or undesirable effects. Thus, it is with the principles of learning. When satisfactorily applied, they can be important in the creative development of the child.

Reducing Stress in Children Through Creative Relaxation is a fine book that explores a very important dimension in the stress field, and I have no hesitation in alerting all parents and educators to its content.

Hans Selye

PREFACE

ALTHOUGH stress is ordinarily thought of as being predominantly concerned with the adult population, undesirable stress can also have a devastating effect on growing children. In this regard, it is interesting to note that of the voluminous amount of literature on stress that has appeared in recent years, in both the scientific community and in popular sources, a relatively small amount of it has been concerned directly with children. Therefore, it is the intent of this book to provide information about stress in childhood for teachers and parents so that they will be able not only to take measures to deal with it but also to try to prevent it as well.

In recent years there have been many techniques used for the purpose of coping with stress. These range from the generally accepted standard procedures to such activities as watching fish swimming in a home aquarium. It has even been recommended by some that petting a dog or a cat can be an effective stress reducer. The stress reduction technique that we have developed is identified as *creative relaxation*. This technique has been field tested with large numbers of children and has been found to be a very effective means of reducing stress.

In most of the chapters of the book the purpose is to provide the reader with valid information about the particular subject at hand, as well as to help him or her convey such information to children. The purpose of the initial chapter is to introduce to the adult reader (teacher and/or parent) some of the various aspects concerned with stress, and to assist the adult in his or her efforts to develop an understanding about stress with children. The second chapter is designed to help the reader understand the emotions of childhood so that he or she will be in a better position to assist children in making satisfactory adjustments to the world around them. Chapter 3 takes into account various aspects that create stressful conditions in children. Included are factors such as self concerns of children and home and school conditions. In chapter 4 there is a detailed discussion about relaxation, particularly as it pertains to stress reduction. The fifth chapter explains the use of creative movement as a medium of learning for children, as well as its function in reducing stress. The final two chapters provide many creative movements that can be used to provide for relaxation of children in a fun-oriented situation. Complete details on the use of these activities are provided for the teacher and/or parent.

The authors wish to extend their sincere appreciation to the many teachers, parents, and children who participated so willingly in our experiments with creative movement as a stress reduction technique for children. A special debt of gratitude is extended to Dr. Hans Selye, the world's foremost authority on the subject of stress, for evaluating certain parts of the book and preparing the foreword. Knowing Dr. Selye has been a very inspirational experience, and we will be eternally grateful for his guidance and counsel in our work in the area of stress as it relates to young children.

A book of this nature should find use as a textbook in professional preparation courses concerned with various aspects of child development. In addition, it should be useful as a supplementary text in courses concerned with stress management. Finally, it could serve as a guide for teachers and parents who wish to provide for stress reduction for children in an interesting and enjoyable way.

J. H. H.
J. N. H.

CONTENTS

Page

Foreword . . . . *v*
Preface . . . . *vii*

Chapter

1. UNDERSTANDING THE STRESS CONCEPT 3
2. CHILDHOOD EMOTIONS 24
3. FACTORS THAT INDUCE STRESS IN CHILDREN 43
4. RELAXATION AND STRESS REDUCTION 62
5. CREATIVE MOVEMENT 80
6. CREATIVE MOVEMENT FOR GENERAL RELAXATION 88
7. CREATIVE MOVEMENT FOR SPECIFIC RELAXATION 107

Index 123

REDUCING STRESS IN CHILDREN THROUGH CREATIVE RELAXATION

Chapter 1

UNDERSTANDING THE STRESS CONCEPT

IN recent years, it has become well-known that what has come to be known as *stress* may be one of the most serious problems facing human beings in modern times. Some recent estimates suggest that as many as 90 percent of all illnesses are in some way stress related.

Although we tend to think of stress as being predominantly concerned with the adult population, it can also have a devastating effect on growing children. Therefore, it is the intent of this book to provide information about stress and children for teachers and parents so that they will be able not only to take measures to deal with it but also to try to prevent it. In this regard, it is interesting to note that of the voluminous amount of literature on stress that has appeared in recent years in both the scientific community and in popular sources, a relatively small amount of it has been concerned directly with children.

In most of the chapters of the book the purpose will be to provide the reader with valid information about the particular subject, as well as to help him or her convey such information to children. In this particular connection, the specific aim of this initial chapter is (1) to convey to the adult reader (teacher and/or parent) some of the various aspects concerned with stress, and (2) to assist the teacher or parent in his or her efforts to develop an understanding about stress for children.

THE PROBLEM OF TERMINOLOGY

There appears to be several important reasons why we should introduce this book with a clarification of terminology involving stress. For one thing, our review of several hundred pieces of literature concerned with stress has revealed that terminology connected with it is not only vast, but sometimes contradictory and, to say the least, rather confusing. Many times, terms whose meanings are different are likely to be used interchangeably to mean the same thing. Conversely, the same term may be used under various circumstances to denote several different meanings. The resulting confusion for a reader is obvious, because such usage of terminology can generate a situation of multiple meanings as far as the general area of stress is concerned. In this regard, our interviews and surveys of large numbers of teachers and others have revealed a wide variety of understandings (or possibly misunderstandings) with reference to the meaning of stress and related terms.

In the discussion of terminology that follows we will try to develop some working descriptions of terms for the purpose of communicating with you, the reader. This means that in no sense are we trying to impose terminology meanings upon you. If you prefer other meanings of these terms, you should feel free to use them in your communication with others.

In some instances, we will resort to terms used by various authorities in the field, and in others, insofar as they may be available, pure technical definitions will be used. It should be understood that many of the terms to which we will allude have some sort of general meaning attached to them. An attempt will be made in some cases to start with this general meaning and give it specificity for the subject at hand. The discussions that follow will take into account the terms *stress, tension, emotion,* and *anxiety.*

Stress

There appears to be little or no solid agreement regarding the derivation of the word *stress.* For example, some sources suggest that the term is derived from the Latin word *stringere,* meaning "to bind tightly." Other sources contend that the term derives from the French word *destresse* (Anglicized to *distress*) and suggest that the prefix "dis" was eventually eliminated due to slurring, as in the case of the word "because" becoming "cause."

A common generalized literal description of the term stress is a "constraining force or influence." When applied to the human organism this could be interpreted to mean the extent to which the body can withstand a given force or influence. In this regard, one of the most often quoted descriptions of stress is that of the famous pioneer in the field, Dr. Hans Selye, President of the International Institute of Stress, who described it as the "nonspecific response of the body to any demand."[1] This means that stress involves a mobilization of the bodily resources in response to some sort of stimulus. These responses can include various physical and chemical changes in the organism. This description of stress could be extended by saying that it involves demands that tax and/or exceed the resources of the human organism. This means that stress not only involves these bodily responses, but that it also involves wear and tear on the organism brought about by these responses. In essence, stress can be considered as any factor acting internally or externally that makes it difficult to adapt and that induces increased effort on the part of the person to maintain a state of equilibrium within himself and with his external environment. It should be understood that stress is a *state* that one is in, and this should not be confused with any *agent (stressor)* that produces such a state.

Tension

Tension is concerned with any unnecessary or exaggerated muscle contractions that could be accompanied by abnormally great or reduced activities of the internal organs. Tensions can be viewed in two frames of reference: (1) as *physiologic* or *unlearned tensions* and (2) as *psychologic* or *learned tensions*.

An example of the first, physiologic or unlearned tensions, would be "tensing" at bright lights or intense sounds. Psychologic, or learned tensions are responses to stimuli that ordinarily do not involve muscular contractions, but that at some time earlier in a person's experience were associated with a situation in which ten-

---

[1] Selye, Hans: *Stress Without Distress*. Scarborough, Ontario, Canada, The New American Library of Canada Limited, 1974, p. 14.

sion was a part of the normal response. Because the brain connects any events that stimulate it simultaneously, it would appear to follow that, depending upon the unlimited kinds of personal experiences one might have, he or she may show tension to any and all kinds of stimuli. An example of a psychologic or learned tension would be an inability to relax when riding in a car after experiencing or imagining too many automobile accidents.

What this means is that physiologic or unlearned tensions are current and spontaneous, while psychologic or learned tensions may be latent as a result of a previous experience and may emerge at a later time. Perhaps the essential difference *between* stress and tension is that the former involves a physical and/or mental state concerned with wear and tear on the organism, while the latter is either a spontaneous or latent condition that can bring about this wear and tear.

Emotion

Because the terms *stress* and *emotion* are used interchangeably in the literature, consideration should be given to the meaning of the latter term. A description of the term *emotion* that we tend to like is one that considers it as the response an individual makes when confronted with a situation for which he is unprepared or that he interprets as a possible source of gain or loss to him. For example, if an individual is confronted with a situation for which he may not have a satisfactory response, the emotional pattern of fear could result. If he finds himself in a position in which his desires are frustrated, the emotional pattern of anger may occur. When viewed in this frame of reference, as some authorities on the subject do, emotion, then, is not the state of stress itself, but rather it is a stressor that can stimulate stress. (The subject of childhood emotion will be discussed in greater detail in the following chapter.)

Anxiety

Another term often used to mean the same thing as stress is *anxiety*. Some of the literature uses the expression "anxiety *or* stress," implying that they are one and the same thing. A basic literal meaning of the term anxiety is "uneasiness of the mind," but this simple generalization may be more complex than one might think. For example, Dr. C. Eugene Walker indicates that psychologists who deal with this area in detail have difficulty in defining the term. He gives as his own description of it the "reaction to a situation where we believe our well-being is endangered or threatened in some way."[2] Dr. David Viscott considers anxiety as the fear of hurt or loss. He contends that this leads to anger with anger leading to guilt, and guilt, unrelieved, leading to depression.[3]

Anxiety should not necessarily be considered the same as stress. Rather, it can be thought of as a combination of certain emotional patterns, principally fear and anger, that can place one in a frame of mind that can bring about stress.

So much for terminology. Although the above discussion of certain terms does not exhaust the vocabulary used in relation to stress, it is hoped that it will serve in part to help the reader distinguish the usage of terms basic to an understanding of the general area of stress. (Other terminology will be described as needed at the time we are dealing with certain specific topics in subsequent discussions in the book.)

TEACHERS' CONCEPTS OF STRESS

Since there is some degree of confusion with reference to the meaning of stress, it might be of interest to teacher-readers to know how teachers in general describe the term. In our extensive studies of the subject we considered it appropriate to try to get some idea of teachers' concepts of it. This was accomplished by having teachers fill in the sentence completion item, Stress is _____. The following discussion is based upon data derived from this source.[4] "Experts" are not in complete agreement as to a precise meaning of it. Our consideration of teachers' concepts of stress focused on the number of times certain *key*

---

[2]Walker, C. Eugene: *Learn to Relax: 13 Ways to Reduce Tension.* Englewood Cliffs, NJ, Prentice-Hall, Inc., 1975, p. 3.

[3]Viscott, David: *The Language of Feelings.* New York, Arbor House, 1976, p. 30.

[4]Humphrey, James H., and Humphrey, Joy N.: *How Teachers Can Cope With Stress.* College Park, Md, James H. Humphrey and Joy N. Humphrey, 1980, p. 32-34.

words emerged in the responses. By identifying such key words, we felt that we could make a fairly valid assessment of how teachers conceived of what stress means to them.

The word *pressure* appeared in 40 percent of the responses. This was by far the most popular key word by almost a two to one margin over all other key words combined. This is interesting because the word *pressure* rarely appears in the literature on stress except when it is used in connection with *blood pressure*. It is also interesting to note that the lead definition of the term pressure in most standard dictionaries considers it in relation to the human organism by referring to pressure as "burden of physical or mental distress."

Some representative examples of how teachers used the word pressure in describing their concept of stress follow:

>   emotional pressure
>   physical and psychological consequences of internal and external pressure
>   working under undue pressure
>   pressure caused by sources known and unknown
>   a feeling of being unable to cope with pressure
>   pressure harmful to health

The key word appearing next most frequently, 15 percent of the time, was *tension*. It may be recalled that we discussed tension in some detail previously, giving consideration to physiologic or unlearned tensions as well as psychologic or learned tensions. We made an arbitrary differentiation between stress and tension at that point.

Most often those teachers who used the term tension in connection with their concept of stress did so in the following manner:

>   a feeling of tension
>   those factors that cause tension
>   tension that is harmful to health
>   tension that occurs as a result of pressure

Following closely behind the word tension was the key word *frustration* used by 13 percent of the respondents as a means of describing their concept of stress. We tend to consider frustration to be a result of one's needs (basic demands) not being met. Thus, stress can be induced as a result of frustration. This means that frustration is not the same as stress but that it becomes a stressor when one is frustrated because his needs are not being met. In any event, many of those teachers who conceived frustration as stress used the term as follows:

>frustration from complying with orders
>frustration in the environment that influences performance
>frustration that results in a mental or emotional state that disrupts routine
>frustration causing inner conflict
>frustration that consumes daily mental activity
>frustration caused by having to do something you don't want to do

In 10 percent of the responses the key word used to express the concept of stress was *strain*. As with the term *pressure*, the word strain is used very little in the literature on stress.

It may be recalled that we mentioned previously that some sources suggest that the word stress is derived from the Latin word *stringere* meaning "to bind tightly." It should be of interest that the word strain also derives from the same Latin word. This being the case, it would be easy to rationalize that stress and strain might be considered as one and the same thing; however, the term strain tends to be used in connection with unusual tension in a muscle caused by overuse or because of a sudden or unaccustomed movement.

Examples of how teachers used the word strain in describing stress were:

>mental strain from problems in a person's environment
>strain caused by a source known or unknown
>strain on physical and mental well-being
>excess strain on the body

The key words *anxiety*, *emotion*, and *fatigue* were each used by 6 percent of the teachers to describe their concept of stress. In our previous description of anxiety it was indicated that it should not be considered the same as stress, but rather that it can be thought of as a combination of certain emotional patterns, principally fear and anger, that can place one in a condition that can bring about stress. Typically, teachers used the term anxiety in connection with their concept of stress as follows:

> demands made on the body caused by anxiety
> an anxiety reaction

As far as the key word emotion is concerned, some British researchers report that the terms stress and emotion are used interchangeably in the literature, presumably to mean the same thing.[5]

As regards their concepts of stress some teachers used the term emotion as follows:

> a positive or negative emotional experience
> upsetting the emotions
> a condition that causes emotional rather than logical reactions
> outside emotional influences

The 6 percent of the respondents who used the term fatigue in expressing their concept of stress, ordinarily described stress as follows:

> unnecessary fatigue caused by unpleasant situations
> that point of mental and physical fatigue beyond human capacity
> continuous bombardment that fatigues an individual

In summarizing the responses from teachers regarding their concepts of stress, two rather interesting bits of information emerged. First, there were relatively few teachers who saw any aspect of stress as positive. That is, the responses were predominantly of a nature that conceived stress as always being undesirable with little or no positive effects. Second, in a large percentage of the cases teachers' concepts of stress tended to focus on the stressor rather than the condition of stress itself. This would appear to be natural, since it has been only in relatively recent years that literature on the subject of stress has become plentiful in terms of describing what it is and how it affects the human organism.

THEORIES OF STRESS

It should perhaps be mentioned at this point that it is not the intent to get into a highly technical discourse on the complex and

---

[5] Brooke, J.D., and Whiting, H.T.A.: *Human Movement — A Field of Study.* London, Henry Kimpton Publishers, 1973, p. 53.

complicated aspects of stress. Nevertheless, there are certain basic understandings that need to be taken into account, and this requires the use of certain technical terms. For this reason, it appears appropriate to provide an "on-the-spot" glossary of terms used in the discussion to follow.

ACTH (*A*dreno*C*ortico*T*ropic *H*ormone) is secreted by the pituitary gland. It influences the function of the adrenals and other glands in the body.

adrenalin A hormone secreted by the medulla of the adrenal glands.

adrenals Two glands in the upper posterior part of the abdomen that produce and secrete hormones. They have two parts, the outer layer called the *cortex* and the inner core called the *medulla*.

corticoids Hormones produced by the adrenal cortex, an example of which is *cortisone*.

endocrine Glands that secrete their hormones into the bloodstream.

hormone A chemical produced by a gland, secreted into the bloodstream, and influencing the function of cells or organs.

hypothalamus The primary activator of the autonomic nervous system, it plays a central role in translating neurological stimuli into endocrine processes during stress reactions.

pituitary An endocrine gland located at the base of the brain about the size of a pea. It secretes important hormones, one of which is the ACTH hormone.

thymus A ductless gland that is considered a part of the endocrine gland system, located behind the upper part of the breast bone.

Although there are various theories concerned with the nature of stress, one of the better known and widely accepted ones is that of the previously mentioned Dr. Hans Selye.[6] We have already given Selye's description of stress as the "nonspecific response of

---

[6] Selye, Hans: *The Stress of Life.* New York, McGraw-Hill, Inc., 1956.

the body to any demand." The physiological processes and the reactions involved in Selye's stress model is known as the *general adaptation syndrome* and consists of the three stages of *alarm reaction, resistance stage,* and the *exhaustion stage.*

In the first stage (alarm reaction) the body reacts to the stressor and causes the hypothalamus to produce a biochemical "messenger" that, in turn, causes the pituitary gland to secrete ACTH into the blood. This hormone then causes the adrenal gland to discharge adrenalin and other corticoids. This causes shrinkage of the thymus with an influence on heart rate, blood pressure, and the like. It is during the alarm stage that the resistance of the body is reduced.

In the second stage, *resistance* develops if the stressor is not too pronounced. Body adaptation develops to fight back the stress or possibly avoid it, and the body begins to repair damage, if any.

The third state of *exhaustion* occurs if there is long-continued exposure to the same stressor. The ability of adaptation is eventually exhausted, and the signs of the first state (alarm reaction) reappear. Selye contends that our adaptation resources are limited, and when they become irreversible, the result is death. (Our objective, of course, should be to keep our resistance and capacity for adaptation.)

As mentioned previously, Selye's stress model that places emphasis upon "nonspecific" responses has been widely accepted. Nevertheless, recently the nonspecific nature of stress has been questioned by some. In this connection, reference is made to the brilliant research of Dr. John W. Mason of Yale, a former President of the American Psychomatic Society. His findings tend to support the idea that there are other hormones involved in stress in addition to those of the pituitary-adrenal system.[7] Dr. Mason's data suggest that psychological stressors activate other endocrine systems besides those activated by physiological stressors such as cold, electric shock, and the like.

As in the case of all research, the search for truth will continue, and more and more precise and sophisticated procedures will emerge in the scientific study of stress. Current theories will be

---

[7]Mason, John W. et al.: Selectivity of corticosteroids and catecholamine responses to various natural stimunli. In Serban, George (Ed.): *Psychopathology of Human Adaptation.* New York, Plenum Publishing Corporation, 1976.

Understanding the Stress Concept

more critically appraised and evaluated and other theories are likely to be advanced. In the meantime, there is abundant evidence to support the notion that stress in modern society is a most serious threat to the well-being of man, if not controlled; of course, the most important factor in such control is man himself.

REACTIONS TO STRESS

There are various ways in which reactions to stress may be classified, and in any kind of classification there will be some degree of unavoidable overlapping. In this discussion we arbitrarily suggest two broad classifications as *physiological* and *behavioral*.

Physiological Reactions

Although all individuals do not always react in the same way *physiologically* as far as stress is concerned, the following generalized list suggests some of the more or less standard body reactions.

1. Rapid beating of the heart, sometimes described as "pounding of the heart." We have all experienced this reaction at one time or another as a result of great excitement, or in the case of being afraid.
2. Perspiration, mostly of the palms of the hands, although there may be profuse sweating in some individuals at various other parts of the body.
3. The blood pressure rises, which may be referred to as a hidden reaction because the individual is not likely to be aware of it.
4. The pupils of the eyes may dilate, and again the individual will not necessarily be aware of this.
5. The stomach seems to "knot up," and we tend to refer to this as "feeling a lump in the pit of the stomach." This, of course, can have a negative influence on digestion.
6. Sometimes individuals experience difficulty in swallowing that is often characterized as a "lump in the throat."
7. There may be a "tight" feeling in the chest and when the stressful condition is relieved one may refer to it as "getting a load off of my chest."

What these various bodily reactions mean is that the organism is gearing up for a response to a stressor. This phenomenon is called the *fight or flight* response and was first described as an *emergency reaction* by Dr. Walter B. Cannon, the famous Harvard professor of physiology a good many years ago. The fight or flight response prepares us for action in the same way that it did for prehistoric man when he was confronted with an enemy. His response was decided on the basis of the particular situation, such as fighting an opponent for food or fleeing from a savage animal that provided him with an overmatched situation.

In modern times with all of the potentially stressful conditions provoking a fight or flight response, modern man uses these same physiological responses to face up to these kinds of situations. Today we generally do not need to fight physically, although we might feel like it sometimes, or run from wild animals, but our bodies still react with the same fight or flight response.

Behavioral Reactions

In discussing *behavioral* reactions it should be mentioned again that various degrees of unavoidable overlapping may occur between these reactions and physiological reactions. Although behavioral reactions are for the most part physically oriented, they are likely to involve more overt manifestations that are provoked by the physiological reactions. For purposes of this discussion we will consider *behavior* to mean anything that the organism does as a result of some sort of stimulation.

A person under stress will function with a behavior that is different than ordinary behavior. We will arbitrarily subclassify these as (1) *counter* behavior (sometimes referred to as defensive behavior), (2) *dysfunctional* behavior, and (3) *overt* behavior (sometimes referred to as expressive behavior).

In *counter* behavior a person will sometimes take action that is intended to counteract the stressful condition. For example, a teacher may counter a situation by shouting at a student who has stimulated a stressful situation by committing an act that is not acceptable to the teacher. Incidentally, some studies show that this kind of behavior on the part of a teacher may be associated with less successful teaching and also that it might make students more disruptive.

Another example of counter behavior is that of an individual taking a defensive position, such as a teacher avoiding a particular unacceptable act of a student. Although this approach can result in the reduction of inappropriate behavior, it may have an adverse affect on the anxiety level of the teacher. For example, if a teacher is already under stress in a given teaching situation, this may become more pronounced when a teacher ignores inappropriate behavior. Of course, this is contingent upon the degree of acceptability of the student behavior.

A final example of counter behavior is the teacher practicing an "on the spot" coping technique, but at the same time being unaware of it. That is, the teacher may take a deep breath and silently "count to ten" before taking action, if any.

Dysfunctional behavior means that a person will react in a manner that demonstrates impaired or abnormal functioning that results in a lower level of skill performance than he is ordinarily capable of accomplishing. There may be changes in the normal speech patterns and there may be a temporary impairment of the systems of perception as well, as temporary loss of memory. Many teachers have experienced this at one time or another due to a stress inducing situation with a "mental block" causing some degree of frustration while attempting to get back on the original train of thought.

Overt behavior involves reactions such as distorted facial expressions like tics and twitches and biting the lip. There appears to be a need for the person to move about, and thus, pacing around the room is characteristic of this condtion. Incidentally, there is strong support for the idea that overt behavior in the form of activity is preferable for most individuals in most stressful situations and can be highly effective in reducing threat and distress.

PHYSICAL AND EMOTIONAL STRESS

There are various ways of classifying stress, but for purposes of this book, we prefer to identify the two broad classifications of physical and emotional stress.

Physical Stress

In discussing physical stress it might be well to differentiate between the two terms *physical* and *physiological*. The former should be considered a broad term and can be described as "pertaining to or relating to the body." The term *physiological* is concerned wih what the organs of the body do in relation to each other. Thus, physical stress could be concerned with unusual and excessive physical exertion as well as certain physiological conditions brought about by some kind of stress.

Although there are many kinds of physical stress, they can perhaps be separated into two general types to which the organism may react in different ways. One type may be referred to as *emergency* stress and the other as *continuing* stress. In emergency stress the previously described physiological phenomenon takes place. That is, when an emergency arises such as a bodily injury, hormones are discharged into the bloodstream. This involves increase in heart rate and rise in blood pressure, along with dilation of the blood vessels in the muscles to prepare themselves for immediate use of the energy that is generated.

In continuing stress, the body reaction is more complex. The physiological involvement is the same, but more and more hormones continue to be produced, the purpose of which is to increase body resistance. In cases in which the stress is excessive, such as an extensive third degree burn, a third phase in the form of exhaustion of the adrenal glands can develop, sometimes culminating in fatal results.

It was mentioned that physical stress can also be concerned with unusual and excessive physical exertion. This can be depicted in a general way by performing an experiment involving some more or less mild physical exertion. First, try to find your resting pulse. This can be done by placing your right wrist, palm facing you, in your left hand. Now, bring the index and middle fingers of your left hand around the wrist and press lightly until you feel the beat of your pulse. Next, time this beat for ten seconds and then multiply this figure by six. This will be your resting pulse rate per minute. For example, if you counted twelve beats in the ten seconds, your resting pulse will be seventy-two beats per minute. The next step is to engage in some physical activity. Stand and balance yourself on one foot. Hop up and down on this foot for a period of about thirty seconds, or less if it is too strenuous. Then take your pulse rate again in the same manner as suggested above. You will find that as a result of this activity your pulse will be elevated above your resting pulse rate. Even with this small amount of physical exertion the body was adjusting to cope with it, as evidence by the rise in pulse rate. This was discernible to you; however, other things, such as a slight rise in blood pressure, of which you were not aware, were likely involved.

Emotional Stress

Emotional stress can be brought about by the stimulus of any of the emotional patterns. For example, the emotional pattern of anger can be stimulated by factors such as the thwarting of one's wishes or a number of cumulative irritations. Responses to such stimuli can be either *impulsive* or *inhibited*. An impulsive expression of anger is one that is directed against a person or an object, while the inhibited expressions are kept under control and may be manifested by such overt behaviors as skin flushing.

Generally speaking, emotional patterns can be placed into the two broad categories of *pleasant* emotions and *unpleasant* emotions. Pleasant emotional patterns include things such as joy, affection, happiness, and love in the broad sense, while included among the unpleasant emotional patterns are anger, sorrow, jealously, fear, and worry — an imaginary form of fear.

At one time or another all of us have manifested emotional behavior as well as ordinary behavior. Differences in the structure of the organism and in the environment will largely govern the degree to which each individual expresses emotional behavior. Moreover, it has been suggested that the pleasantness or unpleasantness of an emotion seems to be determined by its strength or intensity, by the nature of the situation arousing it, and by the way the individual perceives or interprets the situation.

The ancient Greeks identified emotions with certain organs of the body. For example, sorrow was expressed from the heart (a broken heart); jealously was associated with the liver; hate was associated with the gall bladder, and anger was associated with the spleen. As regards the latter, we sometimes hear the expression, "wreaking the spleen" on someone. We make this historical reference because in modern times we take into account certain principal conduits between the emotions and the body. These are by way of the *nervous* system and the *endocrine* system. That part of the nervous system principally concerned with the emotions is the *autonomic* nervous system, which controls functions such as the heart beat, blood pressure, and digestion. When there is a stimulus of any of the emotional patterns these systems activate in the manner previously explained. By way of illustration, if the emotional pattern of fear is stimulated, the heart beat accelerates, breathing is more rapid, and the blood pressure is likely to rise. Energy fuel is discharged into the blood from storage in the liver, which causes the blood sugar level to rise. These, along with other bodily functions, serve to prepare the person to cope with the condition caused by the fear. He then reacts with the fight or flight response discussed earlier in the chapter. (Perhaps, we should interject at this point that the major concern of this book is in the direction of *emotional* stress in children, and this will become more evident in subsequent chapters of the book.)

DESIRABLE STRESS

When stress becomes prolonged and unrelenting, it can result in serious trouble. It is a well-documented fact that emotional upset caused by anger, fear, and the like and stored up over a period of time can be a dangerous threat to health. It has been suggested that what we ordinarily refer to as *aging* is nothing more than the sum total of all the scars left by the stress of life.

In spite of the many undesirable aspects of stress there are certain desirable features of it. The classic comment by Selye that "stress is the spice of life" perhaps sums up the general idea that stress can be desirable as well as devastating. He goes on to say that the only way one could avoid stress would be to never do anything and that certain kinds of activities have a beneficial influence in keeping the stress mechanism in good shape.[8]

Certainly, the human organism needs to be taxed in order to function well, and it is a well-known physiological fact that muscles will soon atrophy if not subjected to sufficient use. It is some-

---

[8] Selye, Hans: *Stress Without Distress.* Scarborough, Ontario, Canada, The New American Library of Canada Limited, 1974, p. 83.;

what like the family car — it will soon rust and deteriorate if left unused. Athletes express a desirable aspect of stress when they talk about the exhilarating feeling of "getting up" for a game and about the feeling of the "juices flowing."

At one time or another, almost all of us have experienced "butterflies in the stomach" when faced with a particularly challenging situation. In the case of a teacher, the excitement of seeing a student learn can be an exhilarating experience and leave one with the joyous feeling of a job well done. In this regard, the famous nineteenth century educator, Horace Mann, once remarked, "I have seen a teacher clap his hands for joy when a boy of 12 has made a bright answer."[9] Thus, it is important that we understand that stress is a perfectly normal human state and that the organism is under various degrees of stress in those conditions that are related to happiness as well as those concerned with sadness and despair.

Some writers have taken the middle ground on this subject by saying that stress is neither good *nor* bad, indicating that the effect of stress is not determined by the stress itself but by how it is viewed and handled, that is, whether we handle stress properly or we allow it to influence us negatively and thus become victims of undesirable stress.[10]

HELPING CHILDREN UNDERSTAND THE STRESS CONCEPT

All of the previous discussions have demonstrated to the reader that the stress concept is complicated and complex. How, then, does one attempt to develop such a complex concept with young children: At first glance this might appear well-nigh impossible. Nevertheless, an extensive project by the present authors has resulted in the production of learning materials designed to help children understand, at least in an elementary way, the concept of stress. The development of this project is reported in detail in the following discussion.

---

[9] Schuessler, Raymond: The man who revolutionized our schools. *NRTA Journal*, Septemper-October, 1977.

---

[10] Culligan, Matthew J., and Sedlacek, *Keith: How to Kill Stress Before It Kills You.* New York, Grosset & Dunlap, Publishers, 1976, pp. 23-24.

In various places in this introductory chapter we have referred to the work of Dr. Hans Selye, one of the most notable scientists of modern times, who is often referred to as the "father of stress." As has been the case with so many stress-related innovations, the germ of the idea for the project reported here originated with Dr. Selye. It came about during some correspondence we were having with him about how teachers can cope with stress. This correspondence revealed that a major interest of Dr. Selye was in the area of developing informational materials that would bring the stress concept down to the level of understanding of young children.

Since the present authors had published a number of children's books and since we had also maintained an interest in stress-related matters, it seemed feasible to explore the possibility of preparing materials about stress for young children. Consequently, we met with Dr. Selye at the International Institute of Stress in Montreal and formulated plans to proceed with the project. At this conference it was decided that the material would be based on the principal behavioral implications of the code of behavior set forth in Dr. Selye's book *Stress Without Distress*. We proceeded in the following manner.

One of our first concerns was to determine how broad the concepts of stress would need to be for satisfactory internalization. We saw a need for collection of data on stress-related experiences of children; that is, we wanted to find out how definitive children would be when considering stressful situations as well as find out their level of understanding about stress. This was accomplished by developing an inquiry instrument that involved a combination of free-response and projective type items. Following are some examples of the items along with some representative responses of children.

    1. How do you feel when you do something nice for someone?

        "I feel nice myself, and I feel happy."
        "I feel good and glad I did it."
        "A good feeling comes over my body."
        "I feel good and will do it again."
        "I feel happy and proud."

    2. How do you feel before you take a test in school?

        "I get a funny feeling in my stomach."

"I feel shaky or something scary."
"I feel nervous and afraid I am going to fail."
"I feel shaky, nervous, and sick."
"I feel like I might sweat or something."

3. How do you feel when you can't do something you want to do?
   "I get mad, and I don't like it."
   "I feel like killing the person who said I couldn't do it."
   "I feel like screaming and throwing a fit."
   "I feel awful, and if I can't do something, I want to try to forget about it."
   "I feel let down."

4. I feel best when _____.
   "I do something right."
   "I do something I always wanted to do."
   "I do something good and make somebody happy."
   "someone cares about me."
   "when I'm with my friends."

5. I feel worst when _____.
   "I'm told I did bad."
   "report cards come out."
   "I've done something wrong."
   "I fail."
   "I work to do something and don't make it."

6. Sadness is _____.
   "not feeling good."
   "being left out."
   "losing your best friend."
   "not being able to do what I want to do."
   "getting something you like taken away."

7. Happiness is _____.
   "being loved."
   "when I learn something new."
   "when school is out."
   "when I get things my way."
   "getting all my work done."

We collected data on over one hundred children through this process and as a result sufficient information was provided to help us determine the extent of the breadth of stress concepts as well as possibilities of internalization of the concepts. This information was also used in discussions with children to help them understand how and why their bodies responded in various ways during happy and unhappy situations.

The next step was the identification of concepts of stress and codes of behavior in *Stress Without Distress* that would be suitable for development with children and that could also be placed in a frame of reference to which they could relate.

With the above information at hand, the next procedure was the development of a thematic scenario to provide a central theme to which children could relate. It was decided that this could best be accomplished by taking a central character (child) through an entire day with supporting characters in the form of parents, peers, a sibling, and a teacher. The environment included the home, school, and play time experiences. A story of approximately 1,500 words was developed in line with this scenario. The application of a standard readability formula placed the reading level of the story at seven years eight months with a two-month measurement error. (A total of twenty-seven picture clues and illustrations that accompany the text tend to reduce the readability appreciably.)

The next undertaking was to try the material out with a large number of children in the age range from six to nine years. Because the reading level was too high for the children in the lower age range, the story was *read* to them. The purpose of the tryout was to determine the extent to which the children could understand the concepts as well as to evaluate their interest in the content.

The tryout was deemed successful, since teachers who observed the children indicated that they displayed considerable interest in the content as compared to other listening and reading materials. Some typical responses of teachers were as follows:

1. "I feel that the story was well written; however, primary children's interest will always dwindle when there are no accompanying illustrations." (As mentioned previously, the story in final form is accompanied by twenty-seven picture clues and illustrations.)
2. "The children maintained an interest throughout the

entire story and participated actively in the discussions that followed."

3. "The children seemed to understand and remember the events in the story."

The final step of the project was to have the material reproduced in a form to be used for widespread distribution to individuals who might wish to try to provide information for young children to help them have a better understanding about stress.[11]

In summary, because the material for this stress-related story for children was scientifically selected, prepared, and tested, it might well be considered unique in the area of children's listening and reading material. To date, the outcomes have been most satisfactory in terms of children's interest in the listening and reading content as well as their understanding of certain broad concepts of stress.

---

[11] The project was produced by Kimbo Educational of Long Branch, New Jersey in 1980 under the title of *Helping Children Understand About Stress*. It consists of a long play recording (listening experience), ten books of the story, *Ted Learns About Stress* (reading experience), and a teacher's manual.

Chapter 2

CHILDHOOD EMOTIONS

AS mentioned in the previous chapter, *emotional stress* of children is the major concern of this book; therefore, it will be important for the reader to be aware of some of the features of childhood emotion.

Dealing with childhood emotions should imply that sympathetic guidance should be provided in meeting anxieties, joys, and sorrows and that help should be given in developing aspirations and security. In order to attempt to reach this objective, we might well consider emotions from a standpoint of the growing child maturing emotionally.

For purposes of this discussion, we will consider *maturity* as being concerned with a state of *readiness* on the part of the organism. The term is most frequently used in connection with age relationships. For example, it may be said that "Johnny is mature for six years of age." Simply stated, *emotional maturity* is the process of acting one's age.

Generally speaking, emotional maturity will be achieved through a gradual accumulation of mild and pleasant emotions. Emotional *immaturity* indicates that unpleasant emotions have accumulated too rapidly for the individual to absorb. One of the important factors in this regard is the process of *adjustment*, which can be described as the process of finding and adopting modes of behavior suitable to the environment or to changes in the environment.

The child's world involves a sequence of experiences that are characterized by the necessity for him to adjust. Consequently, it may be said that "normal" behavior is the result of successful adjustment, and abnormal behavior results from unsuccessful adjustment. The degree of adjustment that the child achieves depends upon how adequately he is able to satisfy his basic needs and to fulfill his desires within the framework of his environment and the pattern or ways dictated by the society.

As mentioned in the first chapter, stress may be considered as any factor acting internally or externally that renders adaptation difficult and that induces increased effort on the part of the person to maintain a state of equilibrium within himself and with his external environment. When stress is induced as a result of the individual's not being able to meet his needs (basic demands) and satisfy his desires (wants or wishes), *frustration* or *conflict* results. Frustration results when a need is not met, and conflict results when (1) choices must be made between nearly equally attractive alternatives or (2) when basic emotional forces oppose one another. In the emotionally healthy person, the degree of frustration is ordinarily in proportion to the intensity of the need or desire. That is, he will objectively observe and evaluate the situation to ascertain whether a solution is possible and, if so, what solution would best enable him to achieve the fulfillment of his needs or his desires. Every person has a "zone of tolerance" or limits for emotional stress within which he normally operates. If the stress becomes considerably greater than the tolerance level or if the individual has not learned to cope with his problems and objectively and intelligently solve them, some degree of maladjustment can possibly result.

In order to counteract some of the above problems and to be able to pursue a sensible course in helping the child become more emotionally mature, there are certain factors concerned with emotional development of children that need to be taken into account. Some of these factors are the subject of the ensuing discussion.

FACTORS CONCERNING EMOTIONAL DEVELOPMENT

Some of the factors concerned with emotional development that need to be considered are (1) characteristics of childhood emotionality, (2) emotional arousals and reactions, and (3) factors that influence emotionality.

Characteristics of Childhood Emotionality

Ordinarily, the emotions of children are not long lasting. A child's emotions may last for a few minutes or less and then terminate rather abruptly. The child gets it "out of his or her system," so to speak, by expressing it outwardly. In contrast, some adult emotions may be long and drawn out. As children get older, expressing the emotions by overt action is encumbered by certain social restraints. This is to say that what might be socially acceptable at one age level is not necessarily so at another. This may be a reason for some children developing *moods*, which in a sense are states of emotion drawn out over a period of time and expressed slowly. Typical moods of childhood may be "sulking" due to restraint or anger, being "jumpy" from repressed fear, and becoming "humorous" from controlled joy or happiness.

The emotions of children are likely to be intense. This might be confusing to some adults who do not understand child behavior; that is, they may not be able to see why a child would react rather violently to a situation that to them might appear insignificant.

The emotions of children are subject to rapid change. A child is capable of shifting rapidly from laughing to crying or from anger to joy. Although the reason for this is not definitely known, it might be that there is not as much depth of feeling among children as there is among adults. In addition, it could be due to the lack of experience that children have had, as well as their state of intellectual development. We do know that young children have a short attention span that could cause them to change rapidly from one kind of emotion to another.

The emotions of children can appear with a high degree of frequency. As children get older, they manage to develop the ability to adjust to situations that previously would have caused an emotional reaction. This is probably due to the child's acquiring more experience with various kinds of emotional situations. Perhaps a child learns through experience what is socially acceptable and what is socially unacceptable. This is particularly true if the child is reprimanded in some way following a violent emotional reaction. For this reason, the child may try to confront situations in ways that do not involve an emotional response.

Children differ in their emotional responses. One child confronted with a situation that instills fear may run away from the immediate environment. Another may hide behind his mother. Still another might just stand there and cry. Different reactions of children to emotional situations are probably due to a host of factors. Included among these may be past experience with a certain kind of emotional situation, willingness of parents and other adults to help children become independent, and family relationships in general.

Strength of children's emotions are subject to change. At some age levels certain kinds of emotions may be weak and later become stronger. Conversely, with some children emotions that were strong may tend to decline. For example, small children may be timid among strangers, but later when they see there is nothing to fear, the timidity is likely to wane.

Emotional Arousals and Reactions

If we are to understand the emotions of children, we need to take into account those factors of emotional arousal and how children might be expected to react to them. Many different kinds of emotional patterns have been identified. For purposes here we have arbitrarily selected for discussion the emotional states of fear, worry, anger, jealousy, and joy.

Fear. It is possible that it is not necessarily the arousal itself but rather the way something is presented that determines whether there will be a fear reaction. For example, if a child is trying to perform a stunt and the discussion is in terms of "If you do it that way you will break your neck," it is possible a fear response will occur. This is one of the many reasons for using a positive approach in dealing with children.

A child may react to fear by withdrawing. With very young children this may be in the form of crying or breath holding. With a child under three years of age and in some older children as well, the "ostrich" approach may be used; that is, he may hide his face in order to get away from it. As children get older, these forms of reactions may decrease or cease altogether because of social pressures. For instance, it may be considered "sissy" to cry, especially among boys. (The validity of this kind of thinking is of course open to question.)

Worry. This might be considered an imaginary form of fear, and it can be a fear not aroused directly from the child's environment. Worry can be aroused by imagining a situation that could possibly arise; that is, a child could worry about not being able to perform well in a certain activity. Since worries are likely to be caused by imaginary rather than real conditions, they are not likely to be found in abundance among very young children. Perhaps the reason for this is that they have not reached a stage of intellectual development at which they might imagine certain things that could cause worry. While children will respond to worry in different ways, certain manifestations such as nail biting may be symptomatic of this condition.

Anger. This emotional response tends to occur more frequently than that of fear. This is probably because there are more conditions that incite anger. In addition, some children quickly learn that anger may get attention that otherwise would not be forthcoming. It is likely that as children get older they may show more anger responses than fear responses because they soon see that there is not too much to fear.

Anger is caused by many factors, one of which is interference with movements the child wants to execute. This interference can come from others or by the child's own limitations in ability and physical development.

Because of individual differences in children, there is a wide variation in anger responses. In general, these responses are either *impulsive* or *inhibited.* In impulsive responses, the child manifests an overt action either toward another person or an object that caused the anger. For instance, a child who collides with a door might take out the anger by kicking or hitting the door. (This form of child behavior is also sometimes manifested by some "adults.") Inhibited responses are likely to be kept under control, and as children mature emotionally, they acquire more ability to control their anger.

Jealousy. This response usually occurs when a child feels a threat of loss of affection. Many psychologists believe that jealousy is closely related to anger. Because of this, the child may build up resentment against another person. Jealousy can be very devastating in childhood, and every effort should be made to avoid it.

Jealousy is concerned with social interaction that involves persons the child likes. These individuals can be parents, siblings, teachers, and peers. There are various ways in which the child may respond. These include (1) being aggressive toward the one of whom he is jealous or possibly toward others as well, (2) withdrawing from the person whose affections he thinks have been lost, and (3) possible development of an "I don't care" attitude.

In some cases children will not respond in any of the above ways. They might try to excel over the person of whom they are jealous or they might tend to do things to impress the person whose affections they thought had been lost.

Joy. This pleasant emotion is one for which we strive because it is so important in maintaining emotional stability. Causes of joy differ from one age level to another and from one child to another at the same age level. This is to say that what might be a joyful situation for one person might not necessarily be so for another.

Joy is expressed in various ways, but the most common are laughing and smiling; the latter being a restrained form of laughter. Some people respond to joy with a state of body relaxation. This is difficult to detect because it has little or no overt manifestation. Nevertheless, it may be noticed when one compares it with body tension caused by unpleasant emotions.

Factors That Influence Emotionality

If we can consider that a child is emotionally fit when his emotions are properly controlled and he is becoming emotionally mature, then emotional fitness is dependent to a certain extent upon certain factors that influence emotionality in childhood. The following is a descriptive list of some of these factors.

Fatigue. There are two types of fatigue, *acute* and *chronic*. Acute fatigue is a natural outcome of sustained or severe exertion. It is due to physical factors such as the accumulation of the by-products of muscular exertion in the blood and to excessive "oxygen debt," the inability of the body to take in as much oxygen as is being consumed by the muscular work. Psychological considerations may also be important in acute fatigue. That is, an individual who becomes bored with his work and who becomes preoccupied with the discomfort involved will become "fatigued" much sooner than if he is highly motivated to do the same work, is not bored, and does not think about the discomfort.

Chronic fatigue has reference to fatigue that lasts over extended periods — in contrast with acute fatigue, which tends to be followed by a recovery phase and restoration to "normal" within a more or less brief period of time. Chronic fatigue may be due to any of a variety of medical conditions ranging from a disease such as tuberculosis to malnutrition. (Such conditions are the concern of the physician who, incidentally, should evaluate all cases of chronic fatigue in order to assure that a disease condition is not responsible). It may also be due to psychological factors such as extreme boredom and/or worry of having to do what one does not wish to do over an extended period.

Fatigue predisposes children to irritability; consequently, we do things to ward it off such as having rest periods or, in the case of the nursery school, fruit juice periods. In this particular regard, some studies show that the hungrier a child is, the more prone he may be to outbursts of anger.

Inferior health status. The same thing holds true here as in the case of fatigue. Temporary poor health, such as colds and the like, tends to make children irritable. There are studies that show that there are fewer emotional outbursts among healthy than unhealthy children.

Intelligence. Studies tend to show that, on the average, children of low intellectual levels have less emotional control than children with higher levels of intelligence. This may be because there may be less frustration if a child is intelligent enough to figure things out. The reverse could also be true because children with high level intelligence are better able to perceive things that would be likely to arouse emotions.

Social environment. In a social environment where such things as quarreling and unrest exist, a child is predisposed to unpleasant emotional conditions. Likewise, school schedules that are too crowded can cause undue emotional excitation among children.

Family relationships. There are a variety of conditions concerned with family relationships that can influence childhood emotionality. Among others, these include (1) parental neglect, (2) overanxious parents, and (3) overprotective parents.

Aspiration levels. It can make an emotionally unstable situation if parent expectations are beyond a child's ability. In addition, children who have not been made aware of their own limitations may set their goals too high and as a result have too many failures.

All of these factors can have a negative influence on childhood emotionality. Therefore, efforts should be made as far as possible to eliminate these factors. Those that cannot be completely eliminated should at least be kept under control.

EMOTIONAL NEEDS OF CHILDREN

It is a very difficult matter to identify specific components of emotional fitness. Therefore, in the absence of such definitive components, we need to look in other directions in our efforts to help children maintain satisfactory levels of emotional fitness. Emotional maturity and, hence, emotional fitness could be expressed in terms of the fulfillment of certain emotional needs.

These needs can be reflected in the developmental characteristics of growing children. A number of emotional characteristics are identified in the following lists at the different age levels. These lists of emotional characteristics have been developed through a documentary analysis of over a score of sources that have appeared in the literature in recent years. It should be understood that these characteristics are suggestive of the behavior patterns of the so-called normal child. This implies that, if a child does not conform to these characteristics, it should not be interpreted to mean that he or she is seriously deviating from the normal. In other words, it should be recognized that each child progresses at his or her own rate and that there will be much overlapping of the characteristics for each of the age levels.

Five-Year-Old Children

1. Seldom show jealousy toward younger siblings.
2. Usually see only one way to do a thing.
3. Usually see only one answer to a question.
4. Inclined not to change plans in the middle of an activity, but would rather begin over.
5. May fear being deprived of mother.

6. Some definite personality traits evidenced.
7. Is learning to get along better, but still may resort to quarreling and fighting.
8. Like to be trusted with errands.
9. Enjoy performing simple tasks.
10. Want to please and do what is expected of them.
11. Are beginning to sense right and wrong in terms of specific situations.

Six-Year-Old Children

1. Restless and may have difficulty in making decisions.
2. Emotional pattern of anger may be difficult to control at times.
3. Behavior patterns may often be explosive and unpredictable.
4. Jealous toward siblings at times; at other times take pride in siblings.
5. Greatly excited by anything new.
6. Behavior becomes susceptible to shifts in direction, inwardly motivated, and outwardly stimulated.
7. May be self-assertive and dramatic.

Seven-Year-Old Children

1. Curiosity and creative desires may condition responses.
2. May be difficult to take criticism from adults.
3. Want to be more independent.
4. Reaching for new experiences and trying to relate to enlarged world.
5. Overanxious to reach goals set by parents and teachers.
6. Critical of self and sensitive to failure.
7. Emotional patterns of anger are more controlled.
8. Becoming less impulsive and boisterous in actions than at six.

Eight-Year-Old Children

1. Dislike taking much criticism from adults.
2. Can give and take criticism in own group.

3. May develop enemies.
4. Do not like to be treated as children.
5. Have a marked sense of humor.
6. First impulse is to blame others.
7. Becoming more realistic and want to find out for themselves.

Nine-Year-Old Children

1. May sometimes be outspoken and critical of adults they know, although they have a genuine fondness for them.
2. Respond best to adults who treat them as individuals and approach them in an adult way.
3. Like recognition for what they have done and respond well to deserved praise.
4. Likely to be backward about public recognition, but like private praise.
5. Developing sympathy and loyalty to others.
6. Do not mind criticism or punishment if they think it is fair, but are indignant if they think it is unfair.
7. Disdainful of danger to and safety of self, which may be a result of increasing interest in activities involving challenges and adventure.

It should be obvious that the above emotional characteristics reflect some of the emotional needs of children at the different age levels. These characteristics should be taken into account if we expect to meet with success in meeting such needs of children.

GUIDELINES FOR EMOTIONAL DEVELOPMENT OF CHILDREN

It is imperative to set forth some guidelines for emotional development if we are to meet with any degree of success in our attempts to provide for emotional development of children. The reason for this is to assure, at least to some extent, that our efforts in attaining optimum emotional development will be based upon a scientific approach. These guidelines might well take the form of valid *concepts of emotional development*. This approach enables us to give serious consideration to what is known about how children grow and develop. The following list of concepts of emotional development with certain implications for the school and/or home environment is submitted with this general idea in mind.

1. *An emotional response may be brought about by a goal's being furthered or thwarted.* The teacher or parent should make a very serious effort to assure successful experiences in the school or home for every child. In the school setting this can be accomplished in part by attempting to provide for individual differences within given school experiences. The school or home setting should be such that each child derives a feeling of personal worth through making some sort of positive contribution.

2. *Self-realization experiences should be constructive.* The opportunity for creative experiences that afford the child a chance for self-realization should be inherent in both home and school. Teachers might well consider planning with children to see that all school activities are meeting their needs and, as a result, involve constructive experience.

3. *Emotional responses increase as the development of the child brings greater awareness and the ability to remember the past and to anticipate the future.* In the school setting the teacher can remind the children of their past emotional responses with words of praise. This could encourage children to repeat such responses in future similar situations and thus provide a better learning situation.

4. *As the child develops, the emotional reactions tend to become less violent and more discriminating.* A well-planned program of school experiences and wholesome home activities should be such that they provide for release of aggression in a socially acceptable manner.

5. *Emotional reactions tend to increase beyond normal expectancy toward the constructive or destructive reactions on the balance of furthering or hindering experiences of the child.* For some children the confidence they need to be able to face the problems of life may come through physical expression. Therefore, experiences such as active play in the home surroundings and good physical education programs in the schools have

tremendous potential to help contribute toward a solid base of total development.

6. *Depending on certain factors, a child's own feelings may be accepted or rejected by the individual.* Children's school and home experiences should make them feel good and have confidence in themselves. Satisfactory self-concept is closely related to body control; physical activity oriented experiences might be considered as one of the best ways of contributing to it. Therefore, it is important to consider those kinds of experiences for young children that will provide them with the opportunity for a certain degree of freedom of movement.

OPPORTUNITIES FOR EMOTIONAL DEVELOPMENT IN THE HOME AND SCHOOL ENVIRONMENT

The school and home have the potential to provide for emotional stability. The extent to which this actually occurs is dependent primarily on the kind of emotional climate provided by the teacher and the parent in the school and home. For this reason, it appears pertinent to examine some of the potential opportunities that exist for emotional development in both the school and home situations. The following descriptive list is submitted for this purpose. It should be borne in mind that these opportunities will not accrue automatically, but that both teachers and parents need to work constantly to try to make such conditions a reality.

1. *Release of aggression in a socially acceptable manner.* This appears to be an outstanding way in which school activities such as physical education can help to make children more secure and emotionally stable. For example, kicking a ball in a game of kickball, batting a softball, or engaging in a combative stunt can afford a socially acceptable way of releasing aggression. The same can be said for a home environment where parents provide their children with wholesome recreation and active play opportunities.

2. *Inhibition of direct response of unpleasant emotions.* This statement does not necessarily mean that feelings concerned with such unpleasant emotions as fear and

anger should be completely restrained. On the contrary, the interpretation should be that such feelings can take place less frequently in a wholesome school and home environment. This means that opportunities should be provided to relieve tension rather than to aggravate it.

3. *Promotion of pleasant emotions.* Perhaps there is too much concern with suppressing unpleasant emotions and not enough attention given to promotion of pleasant ones. This means that the school and home should provide a range of activities by which all children can succeed. Thus, all children, regardless of ability, should be afforded the opportunity for success, at least most of the time.

4. *Recognition of one's abilities and limitations.* It has already been mentioned that a wide range of activities should provide an opportunity for success for all. This should make it easier in the school setting to provide for individual differences of children so that all of them can progress within the limits of their own skill and ability.

5. *Understanding about the ability and achievements of others.* In the school experience emphasis can be placed upon achievements of the group, along with the function of each individual in the group. Team play and group effort is important in most school situations.

6. *Being able to make a mistake without being ostracized.* In the school setting this requires that the teacher serve as a catalyst who helps children understand the idea of trial and error. Emphasis can be placed on *trying* and that one can learn not only from his own mistakes but also from the mistakes of others.

This discussion includes just a few examples of the numerous opportunities to help provide for emotional development in the school and home environment. The resourceful and creative teacher or parent should be able to expand this list manyfold.

IMPLICATIONS OF RESEARCH IN EMOTIONAL BEHAVIOR OF CHILDREN

Over the years, attempts have been made to study various aspects of childhood emotions. A recent undertaking by the National Institute of Education provides some information that might be useful.[1]

The purpose of this report was to provide preschool and early elementary school teachers with a summary of current psychological research concerned with the social development of young children. In submitting the report, the authors noted that caution should prevail with reference to basic research and practical implications. In this regard, the following suggestions are submitted:

1. What seems "true" at one point in time often becomes "false" when new information becomes available or when new theories change the interpretation of the old findings.
2. Substantial problems arise in any attempt to formulate practical suggestions for professionals in one discipline based on research findings from another discipline.
3. Throughout the report, recommendations for teachers have been derived from logical extensions of experimental findings and classroom adaptations of experimental procedures.
4. Some of the proposed procedures may prove unworkable in the classroom, even though they may make sense from a psychological perspective.
5. When evaluating potential applications of psychological findings, it is important to remember that psychological research is usually designed to derive probability statements about the behavior of groups of people.
6. Individual teachers may work better with a procedure that is, on the average, less effective.

The following is a list of generalizations derived from the findings reported in the study of *aggression* in children, and accompanied by possible general implications for the school or home environment. These implications are suggestive only, and the reader will no doubt be able to draw his or her own implications and make practical applications that apply to particular situations.

1. *Children rewarded for aggression learn that aggression pays off.* This generalization is concerned with the ex-

---

[1] Roedell, W., Slaby, R.G., and Robinson, H. B.: *Social Development in Young Children, A Report for Teachers.* Washington, DC, National Institute of Education, U. S. Department of Health, Education and Welfare, January, 1976.

tent to which a teacher or parent uses praise for achievement. The teacher must be able to quickly discern whether success was due more to aggressive behavior than skill or ability. The important thing here is the extent of aggressive behavior. Certainly a teacher should not thwart enthusiasm. It is sometimes difficult to determine whether an act was due to genuine enthusiasm or to overt undesirable aggressive behavior.

2. *Children involved in constructive activities may be less likely to behave aggressively.* In the school setting, this implies that lessons should be well-planned so that time is spent on constructive learning activities. When this is accomplished, it will be more likely that desirable and worthwhile learning will take place.

3. *Children who have alternative responses readily available are less likely to resort to aggression to get what they want.* This is concerned essentially with teacher-child or parent-child relationships. While the school environment generally involves group situations, there are many "one-on-one" opportunities between teacher and child. (This situation pertains as well to the home environment if a parent is willing to spend time on these one-on-one relationships.) This gives the teacher a chance to verbalize to the child the kind of behavior that is expected under certain conditions. For example, a child who *asks* for an object such as a ball is more likely to receive cooperation. A child who *grabs* an object is more likely to elicit retaliatory aggression. Teacher reinforcement can increase children's use of nonaggressive solutions to interpersonal problems.

The teacher should be ready to intervene in a potentially aggressive situation before aggression occurs, encouraging children to use nonaggressive methods to solve conflicts. The teacher can provide verbal alternatives for those children who do not think of them. For example, "I am playing with this now," or "You can ask him to trade with you."

4. *Children imitate behavior of people they like, and they often adopt a teacher's behavior.* Teachers are more likely to be a model adopted by children than would be the

case with most other adults, sometimes including parents. One of the reasons is that many children like to try to please their teachers and tend to make serious efforts to do so. Of course it is helpful if a teacher is nonaggressive in his or her own behavior.
5. *Cooperation may be incompatible with aggression.* This could be interpreted to mean that a teacher or parent should consistently attend to and reinforce all cooperative behavior. Children consistently reinforced for cooperative behavior are likely to increase cooperative interactions while simultaneously decreasing aggressive behavior.

EVALUATING INFLUENCES OF THE ENVIRONMENT ON EMOTIONAL DEVELOPMENT

What we are essentially concerned with here is how an individual teacher or parent can make some sort of valid evaluation of the extent to which the school or home environment contributes to emotional development. This means that the teacher or parent should make some attempt to assess school and home experiences with reference to whether or not these experiences are providing for emotional maturity.

One such approach would be to refer back to the list of opportunities for emotional development in the school and home environment suggested previously in this chapter. These opportunities have been converted into a rating scale as follows and may be used by a teacher and/or parent.

1. The school/home experiences provide for release of aggression in a socially acceptable manner.

    4 most of the time
    3 some of the time
    2 occasionally
    1 infrequently

2. The school/home experiences provide for inhibition of direct response of unpleasant emotions.

    4 most of the time
    3 some of the time
    2 occasionally
    1 infrequently

3. The school/home experiences provide for promotion of pleasant emotions.
    4 most of the time
    3 some of the time
    2 occasionally
    1 infrequently
4. The school/home experiences provide for recognition of one's abilities and limitations.
    4 most of the time
    3 some of the time
    2 occasionally
    1 infrequently
5. The school/home experiences provide for an understanding about the ability and achievement of others.
    4 most of the time
    3 some of the time
    2 occasionally
    1 infrequently
6. The school/home experiences provide for being able to make a mistake without being ostracized.
    4 most of the time
    3 some of the time
    2 occasionally
    1 infrequently

If a teacher or parent makes these ratings objectively and conscientiously, a reasonably good procedure for evaluation is provided. Ratings can be made periodically to see if positive changes appear to be taking place. Ratings can be made for a single experience, a group of experiences, or for the total school or home experience. This procedure can help the teacher or parent identify the extent to which school or home experiences and/or conditions under which the experiences take place are contributing to emotional development.

THE EMOTIONALLY HEALTHY PERSON

It seems appropriate to close this chapter by mentioning some of the characteristics of emotionally healthy persons — teachers and parents, as well as children. As we look at some of these characteristics we must recognize that they are neither absolute nor are they static. We are not always happy, and we sometimes find ourselves in situations in which we are not overly confident. Sometimes we may feel downright inadequate to solve certain commonplace problems that occur in our daily lives.

1. Emotionally healthy persons have achieved basic harmony within themselves and a workable relationship with others. They are able to function effectively, and usually happily, even though they are well aware of the limitations and rigors involved in human existence.
2. Emotionally healthy persons manage to adapt to the demands of environmental conditions with emotional responses that are appropriate in degree and kind to the stimuli and situations and that fall, generally, within the range of what is considered "normal," within the school and home environment.
3. Emotionally healthy persons face problems directly and seek realistic and plausible solutions to them. They try to free themselves from excessive and unreal anxieties, worries, and fears even though they are aware that there is much to be concerned with and much to be anxious about in our complex modern society.
4. Emotionally healthy persons have developed a guiding philosophy of life and have a set of values that are acceptable to themsleves and that are generally in harmony with those values of society which are reasonable and conducive to human happiness.
5. Emotionally healthy persons accept themselves and are willing to deal with the world as it exists in reality. They accept what cannot be changed at a particular time and place, and they build and derive satisfaction within the framework of their own potentialities and those of their environment.
6. Emotionally healthy persons tend to be happy, and they tend to have an enthusiasm for living. They do not focus their attention exclusively upon what they consider to be their inadequacies, weaknesses, and "bad" qualities. They view those around them in this way, too.

7. Emotionally healthy persons have a variety of satisfying interests and maintain a balance between their work, routine responsibilities, and recreation. They find constructive and satisfying outlets for creative expression in the interests that they undertake.

This list of characteristics of emotionally healthy persons presents a near ideal situation, and obviously, none of us operate at these high levels at all times. Nevertheless, they might well be considered as suitable guidelines for which teachers and parents might strive to assist themselves and their children in dealing with and possibly preventing unpleasant emotional stress.

Chapter 3

FACTORS THAT INDUCE STRESS IN CHILDREN

MOST children encounter a considerable amount of stress in our complex modern society. The objectives of those adults who deal with children should be to help them to reduce stress by making a change in the environment and/or making a change in the children themselves. We have already said that each person has a "zone of tolerance" level as far as stress is concerned and that, if the stress becomes considerably greater than the tolerance, a person will suffer from emotional distress and its consequent unhappy circumstances.

One of the problems of stress in children is that they are not likely to be as able to cope with it as adults. The reason for this is that they do not have the readily available options that adults might have. Dr. Margaret Holland, a prominent child psychologist, makes the following comparisons between choices in coping with stress open to children and adults.[1]

1. An open display of anger is often considered unacceptable for children. For example, a teacher can be angry with a student, but children may not have the same right to be angry with a teacher.
2. Adults have the latitude of withdrawing or walking out, but this same option of freedom may not be available to children.
3. It is the belief of some child psychologists that *daydreaming* is therapeutic and productive. At the same

---

[1] Report on a Proseminar Institute in Washington, DC, *The Washington Post,* June 13, 1980.

time, children may be reprimanded for "daydreaming" in school.
4. An adult can get a prescription for "nerves" from a physician — another option not available to children.

It is very likely that more often than not children may be punished for using some of the same kinds of stress coping techniques that are satisfactory for adults. Yet, some of these behaviors are considered socially unacceptable as far as children are concerned.

Indeed, the average child's environment abounds with many stress inducing factors — society in general, the home, and the school. Things such as various kinds of teacher and parent behaviors can have frustrating influences on children. A major function of this chapter is to identify and elaborate on some of the factors that induce stress in children. When teachers and parents are more aware of some of these factors, perhaps they can try to alleviate some of them and also try to help children deal with those situations that are difficult to eliminate.

SELF CONCERNS OF CHILDREN THAT CAN INDUCE STRESS

One of the important classifications of stress inducing factors in children is that that involves *personal* or *self* concerns. The following generalized descriptive list takes some of these factors into account.

1. *Self concerns associated with the meeting of personal goals.* Stress is likely to result if adults set goals for children that are too difficult for them to accomplish. For example, goals may be much higher than a particular school or home environment will permit children to achieve. On the contrary, when goals are set too low, children may develop the feeling that they are not doing as much for themselves as they should. This aspect of stress is also concerned with the fear that some children have that they will not reach their goals in life. It is interesting to note that this can sometimes happen early in a child's life.
2. *Self concerns that involve self-esteem.* This involves the way one feels about himself, and one's self-esteem can often be highly related to the fulfillment of certain *ego needs*. Some children may feel that there are not enough

opportunities offered in modern society for them to succeed. This is perhaps more true of those children who are in a low socioeconomic environment. It bothers some children, too, that adults do not praise them for what they consider to be a job well done.

3. *Self concerns related to changing values.* It is frustrating to some children if they do not understand the value system imposed on them in a given school environment. They may develop the feeling that adults are not inclined to place a value on those factors which children feel are important to them personally at their various stages of growth and development.

4. *Self concerns that center around social standards.* In some cases children get confused with the difference in social standards required at the different levels of their development. It is sometimes difficult for them to understand that what was socially acceptable at one age level is not necessarily so at another.

5. *Self concerns involving personal competence and ability.* This is probably the self concern that frustrates children the most. Certainly, lack of confidence in one's ability can be devastating to the morale of a child. Many children are becoming increasingly concerned with their ability, or lack thereof, to cope with problems such as expectations of parents and keeping up with school work.

6. *Self concerns about their own traits and characteristics.* Certainly not the least of the concerns among children are those factors which are likely to make them different from the so-called average or normal child. This is concerned with the social need for *mutuality,* which means their wanting to be like their peers. When children deviate radically from others in certain traits and characteristics, it can be a serious stress inducing factor. A specific example is the child who is extremely overweight. Some child psychiatrists feel that they are likely to mature into overweight adults and are more vulnerable to the emotional stress of being fat than adults. Some studies show that overweight children may get

lower grades in school, that in some cases they may be discriminated against by teachers, and that they often have poor social skills.

It should be mentioned that all of these self concerns are not characteristic of all children, particularly because of the individual differences among them. That is, what may be a serious self concern for one child may be a minimal concern for another.

HOME CONDITIONS THAT CAN INDUCE STRESS

Changes in society with consequent changes in conditions in some homes are likely to make child adjustment a difficult problem. Factors such as changes in standards of female behavior, larger percentages of both parents working, economic conditions, mass media such as television, as well as numerous others can complicate the life of the modern-day child.

Some child psychiatrists are convinced that some home conditions can have an extremely negative influence on the personality and mental health of some children. Studies show that the interaction of stress factors is especially important. Most of these studies tend to identify the following factors to be strongly associated with childhood psychiatric disorders: (1) severe marital discord, (2) low social status, (3) over-crowding or large family size, (4) paternal criminality, (5) maternal psychiatric disorder, and (6) admission into the care of local authorities.[2]

It is estimated that with only one of the above conditions present, a child is no more likely to develop psychiatric problems than any other child; however, when two of the conditions occur the child's psychiatric risk increases fourfold.

In our own studies, we found that there were certain actions of parents that induced stress in teachers, and according to the teachers, these parental attitudes might well be considered as stress inducing factors for their students.[3]

---

[2] Rutter, Michael: Some grow up undisturbed: Why? *The Spectrum*. Iowa City, IA, University of Iowa, Winter, 1977.

---

[3] Humphrey, James H., and Humphrey, Joy N.: *How Teachers Can Cope With Stress.* College Park, MD, James H. Humphrey and Joy N. Humphrey, 1980, p. 42.

Actions of parents that induce stress in teachers can be classified into three areas: (1) lack of concern of parents for their children, (2) parental interference, and (3) lack of parental support for teachers.

In 45 percent of the cases, *lack of parental concern for children* was stressful for teachers. They cited things such as parents not caring when a student did poorly, parents not being willing to help their children with school work, a lack of home discipline, and stress placed on teachers by the difficult time they had in getting parents to conferences.

Thirty-two percent of the teachers saw *parental interference* as a stressor for them. Such interference was often a result of parents having expectations too high for their children. This in turn resulted in parental pressure on children, particularly for grades, which may be one of the most serious conditions in our schools today. Incidentally, in this general connection, it is interesting to note that one authoritative source suggests that attitudes acquired during youth can affect the way an individual reacts to stress as an adult. This may be significant in the case of persons whose family has emphasized performance and achievement to the exclusion of all other characteristics.[4]

It has been suggested that pressure exerted by parents for grades could be a contributing cause of the increase in the suicide rate among students. Moreover, there are some who believe that parents are literally "driving their children to drink" because of an increase in alcohol consumption by children possibly due to the "grade pressure syndrome."

The third classification of parental actions causing stress for teachers was that of *lack of parental support*, and 23 percent identified stress inducing factors here. They were stressed by factors such as not being backed by parents and a general poor attitude of parents toward teachers.

Another, and very important home condition that can induce stress in children is when a family itself is under stress. Parenting itself is an extremely difficult task, and the demands of this task are becoming more and more complicated. Consequently, many of

---

[4]Pellitier, Kenneth R.: *Mind As Healer/Mind As Slayer.* New York, Del Publishing Co., Inc., 1977, p. 104.

the pressures that modern parents are called upon to endure cannot only cause stress for them but can also cause them to induce stress upon their children as well.

A recent publication by the United States Department of Health and Human Services entitled *Families in Stress*[5], suggests that parents who begin to feel that stress of being uptight because of their children ask themselves the following questions:

1. Is it so important that the child *always* do things my way?
2. Can I let the children have it their own way sometimes?
3. Do I really take enough time to try to understand what the children are saying to me?
4. Do I really know what the children want and need from me?
5. Is what I say or tell them to do really clear to them?

In addition to these criteria for the parent's evaluation for dealing with their children the following "stress and tension relievers" are recommended:

1. Count to ten, put the child in a safe area (crib, playpen, childproof room), and go to another room or outside for a few minutes.
2. Go into another room, close the door, and cry or scream. Then take ten minutes to read, knit, or do whatever relaxes you best.
3. Lie on the floor with your feet up on a chair; place a cool washcloth on your face; and think of the most peaceful scene you can imagine. Stay there for five minutes.
4. Tell your child exactly what is making you feel angry. Be really specific about what behavior needs to be changed in order to reduce your anger level.
5. After you've put the child down for a nap, forget what you "should" be doing. Take some time for yourself to relax — sleep, read, listen to music, take a bath — whatever makes you feel fresh again.

---

[5] Johnston, Carol A. *Families in Stress.* Washington, DC, U. S. Department of Health, and Human Services, Publication No. (OHDS) 80-30162, 1979.

6. Designate a corner, chair, or some quiet spot as a "time-out" place where you can go when you feel like losing your temper. Designate a separate one for your child. It gives both of you a few minutes to calm down, *and* it tells the other person that you are getting angry.
7. Save a special, quiet plaything to be used only at certain times. It will be a treat for your child and will provide some quiet time for you.

It is estimated that one million or more children are abused or neglected by their parents or other "overseers" in our country annually, and that as many as two thousand die as a result of maltreatment. Authorities suggest that most of this is not caused by inhuman, hateful intent on the part of parents but rather, it is the result of a combination of factors including the accumulation of stresses on families and the unmet needs of parents for support in coping with their child-rearing responsibilities.

SCHOOL ANXIETIES THAT CAN INDUCE STRESS

There are a number of conditions existing in most schools that can raise stress levels in students. Several of these will be considered in the subsequent discussions of this section of the chapter.

Stress and the Child in the Educational Process

School anxiety as a child stressor is a phenomenon with which educators, particularly counselors and teachers, frequently find themselves confronted in dealing with children. Various theories have been advanced to explain this phenomenon and relate it to other character traits and emotional dispositions. Literature on the subject reveals the following characteristics of anxiety as a stress inducing factor in the educational process.

1. Anxiety is considered a learnable reaction that has the properties of a response, a cue of danger, and a drive.
2. Anxiety is internalized fear aroused by the memory of painful past experiences associated with punishment for the gratification of an impulse.
3. Anxiety in the classroom interferes with learning, and whatever can be done to reduce it should serve as a spur to learning.

4. Test anxiety is a near universal experience, especially in this country, which is a test-giving and test-conscious culture.
5. Evidence from clinical studies points clearly and consistently to the disruptive and distracting power of anxiety effects over most kinds of thinking.

It would seem that causes of anxiety change with age as do perceptions of stressful situations. Care should be taken in assessing the total life space of the child — background, home life, school life, age, and sex — in order to minimize the anxiety experienced in the school. It seems obvious that school anxiety, although manifested in the school environment, may often be caused by unrelated factors outside the school.

Test Anxiety as a Stress Inducing Factor

A few years ago The Society for Research in Child Development released two monographs that contained extensive longitudinal studies on test anxiety as it relates to school children.[6]

The first study represented a limited attempt to determine the relation over time between anxiety and indices of intellectual and academic performance. The following three major results were revealed:

1. The expected negative correlation between test anxiety and IQ tends to be small and insignificant in the first year, but increases significantly in the negative direction over time.
2. These tendencies are more marked and significant when measures designed to correct for sources of distortion of self-report are used.
3. The strength of the negative correlations between test anxiety and IQ scores are consistently stronger when third grade rather than first grade test anxiety scores are used as the predictor variable.

The second study is the summation of a longitudinal study of defensiveness to intelligence and achievement test performance

---

[6] Hill, K. T., and Sarasen, S. B.: *The Relation of Test Anxiety and Defensiveness to Test and School Performance Over the Elementary School Years*. Monograph of the Society for Research in Child Development, 31 (2, Serial No. 104), 1966.

and of school progress over the elementary school years. Some of the major findings indicated the following:

1. There was an increasingly negative relationship between anxiety and test performance over the entire elementary school experience.
2. Anxiety was greater on verbal than on nonverbal tests.
3. Unfamiliar tests aroused much anxiety.

In addition to the above reports, a great deal of research has appeared on test anxiety in various sources over the years. One literature review on the subject suggests the following generalizations.[7]

1. A critical factor is what the test situation means to a particular individual in terms of his learned patterns of response to anxiety. If the test is considered important to the individual and if he is anxious when taking tests, he is more likely to perform poorly on tests than one who is less anxious.
2. There is a negative relationship between level of ability and level of anxiety. Poorer students tend to be most anxious when facing a test.
3. There is a positive correlation between level of anxiety and level of aspiration. Those who are least anxious when facing a test tend to be those who have the least need or desire to do well in it.
4. Extreme degrees of anxiety are likely to interfere with test performance; however, mild degrees of anxiety facilitate test performance.
5. The more familiar a student is with tests of a particular type, the less likely he is to suffer extreme anxiety.
6. Test anxiety can enhance learning if it is distributed at a relatively low level throughout a course of instruction rather than being concentrated at a relatively high level just prior to and during a test.
7. There are low to moderate negative relationships between measures of anxiety and performance on very complex tasks. This negative relationship tends to increase as the task becomes more test-like.

---

[7]Kirkland, M. C.: The effect of tension on students and schools. *Review of Educational Research*, 41: 303-350, 1971.

8. Test anxiety increases with grade level and appears to be long range rather than transitory.

What then does the nature of test anxiety imply for educational goals and practice? Perhaps there should be a continuing opportunity for all school personnel and parents to report on their experiences with the tests that have been used. This feedback should also place a great deal of emphasis on the students' reactions to their testing experience. It is essential that the reactions of children that give evidence of emotional disturbance in relation to tests be carefully noted and considered, especially when test results are interpreted and used for instructional, guidance, and administrative purposes.

TEACHER BEHAVIORS THAT INDUCE STRESS IN STUDENTS

In the literature much emphasis has been placed on those factors which induce stress in teachers. It certainly seems appropriate to examine behaviors of teachers that tend to induce stress in students. The major reason for this, of course, is that teacher behaviors could possibly have a serious negative effect on those they teach. This is not a recent concern because over two decades ago, on the basis of minimum incidence statistics and pupil-teacher ratios, it was estimated that anxiety may affect as many as 200 thousand and that through them 5 million students may be affected.[8]

Equally important, if teachers induce stress in students, the students, in turn, are likely to manifest behaviors that become stress inducing factors for teachers, and thus, the *vicious circle* is allowed to perpetuate.

Perhaps, one of the most satisfactory ways of identifying teacher behaviors that are likely to cause stress among students is to simply ask the students. In this regard, we recently conducted a study with fifth-and sixth-grade children.[9] A question raised

---

[8] Kaplan, C.: *Mental Health and Human Relations.* New York, Harper and Row, 1959.

---

[9] Humphrey, Joy N., and Humphrey, James H.: *Incidents in the School Environment Which Induce Stress in Upper Elementary School Children.* College Park, MD, Humphrey and Humphrey, 1977.

with 200 fifth-and sixth-grade boys and girls was "What is the one thing that worries you most in school?" As might be expected, there was a wide variety of responses. Nevertheless, the one general characteristic that tended to emerge was the emphasis that teachers placed on *competition* in so many school situations. Although students did not state this specifically, the nature of their responses clearly seemed to be along these general lines.

Certainly there are many conditions in the school situation that, if not carefully controlled, can cause *competitive stress*. This condition has been described as occurring when a child feels (perceives) that he will not be able to respond adequately to the performance demands of competition. When the child feels this way, he experiences considerable threat to self-esteem that results in stress. Moreover, competitive stress is a negative emotion that a child experiences when he perceives the competition to be personally threatening.[10]

Whenever possible, teachers might try to guard against those conditions which may result in competitive stress and at the same time emphasize those kinds of conditions which will more likely promote *cooperation*. In this regard, it is interesting to note that the terms *cooperation* and *competition* are antonymous; therefore, the reconciliation of children's competitive needs and cooperative needs is not an easy matter. In a sense, we are confronted with an ambivalent condition that, if not handled carefully, could place children in a state of conflict. This was recognized by Karen Horney many years ago when she indicated that, although everything is done to spur us toward success, which means that we must not only be assertive but also be aggressive, able to push others out of the way, we are deeply imbued with ideals that declare that it is selfish to want anything for ourselves and that we should be humble, turn the other hand and be yielding.[11] Thus, modern society rewards not only one kind of behavior (cooperation) but also its direct opposite (competition). Perhaps more often than not our

---

[10] Scanlan, Tara K., and Passer, Michael W.: *The Psychological and Social Affects of Competition.* Los Angeles, 1977.

---

[11] Horney, Karen: *The Neurotic Personality of Our Times.* New York, W. W. Norton & Company, Inc., 1937.

cultural demands sanction these rewards without provision of clear-cut standards of value as regards specific conditions under which these forms of behavior might well be practiced. Hence, the child is placed in somewhat of a quandary about when to compete and when to cooperate.

In generalizing on the basis of the available evidence as regards the subject of competition, it seems justifiable to formulate the following concepts:
1. Very young children are not very competitive but become more competitive as they grow older.
2. There is a wide variety in competition among children; that is, some are violently competitive, while others are mildly competitive, and still others are not competitive at all.
3. Boys tend to be more competitive than girls.
4. Competition should be adjusted so that there is not a preponderant number of winners over losers.
5. Competition and rivalry produce results in effort and speed of accomplishment.[12]

With children of elementary school age, at least, teachers might well be guided by these concepts. It should be kept uppermost in mind by both parents and teachers that competition should not be restrained, but kept under control so that competitive needs of children are met in a satisfactory and wholesome way.

SEX DIFFERENCES IN EARLY SCHOOL SUCCESS

In general, emotional stress seems to have a greater effect on boys than on girls in both the school and home environment. One possible exception to this in the school situation is that girls are prone to suffer more anxiety over report cards than are boys. Most studies show that boys are much more likely to be stressed by family discord and disruption than are girls, although there does not seem to be a completely satisfactory explanation for this.

In any event, it is interesting to note that many people have been critical of the early school learning environment, particularly

---

[12] Humphrey, James H., and Humphrey, Joy N.: *Child Learning*, 2nd edition. Dubuque, IA, William C. Brown Company Publishers, 1974, p. 107.

as far as boys are concerned. Some of these critics have gone so far as to say that young boys are being discriminated against in their early school years. Let us examine the premise.

A generally accepted description of the term *learning* is that it involves some sort of change in behavior. Many learning theorists maintain that behavior is a product of heredity and environment. Unquestionably, it is very apparent that environment plays a major role in determining one's behavior. B. F. Skinner, the renowned Harvard University learning theorist has said that man is, indeed, controlled by his environment. Nevertheless, we must remember that it is an environment largely of his own making. The issue here is whether or not an environment is provided that is best suited for learning for boys at the early school grade levels, and further whether such an environment is likely to cause more stress among young boys than young girls.

While the school has no control over ancestry, it can, within certain limitations, exercise some degree of control over the kind of environment in which the learner must function. Generally speaking, it is doubtful that all schools have provided an environment that is most conducive to learning as far as young boys are concerned. Many child development specialists have characterized the environment at the primary level of education as *feminized*.

A major factor to consider is that that concerns the biological differences between boys and girls in this particular age range, and it is questionable whether educational planning has always taken these important differences into account. Over the years there has been an accumulation of evidence on this general subject appearing in the literature on child development, some of which will be summarized here.

Due to certain male hormonal conditions, boys tend to be more aggressive, restless, and impatient. In addition, the male has more rugged bone and muscular structure and as a consequence greater strength than the female at all ages. Because of this, males tend to display greater muscular reactivity that in turn expresses itself in a stronger tendency toward restlessness and vigorous overt activity. This condition is concerned with the greater oxygen consumption required to fulfill the male's need for increased energy production. The male organism might be compared to an engine that operates at higher levels of speed and intensity than the less energetic female organism.

Another factor to take into account is the difference in Basal Metabolic Rate (BMR) in young boys and girls. The BMR is indicative of the speed at which body fuel is changed into energy, as well as how fast this energy is used. The BMR can be measured in terms of calories per meter of body surface with a calorie representing a unit measure of heat energy in food. It has been found that on average BMR rises from birth to about three years of age and then starts to decline until the ages of approximately twenty to twenty-four. The BMR is higher for boys than for girls, particularly at the early age levels. Because of the higher BMR, boys in turn will have a higher amount of energy to expend. Because of differences in sex hormonal conditions and Basal Metabolic Rate, it appears logical to assume that these factors will influence the male in his behavior patterns.

From a growth and developmental point of view, while at birth the female is from one-half to one centimeter less in length than the male and around three hundred grams less in weight, she is actually a much better developed organism. It is estimated on the average that at the time of entrance into school, the female is usually six to twelve months more physically mature than the male. As a result, girls may be likely to learn earlier how to perform tasks of manual dexterity such as buttoning their clothing. In one of our own observational studies of preschool children, it was found that little girls were able to perform the task of tying their shoe laces at a rate of almost four times that of little boys.

Although all schools should not be categorized in the same manner, many of them have been captured by the dead hand of tradition and ordinarily provide an environment that places emphasis upon factors such as neatness, orderliness, and passiveness which it is easier for girls to conform than boys. Of course, this may be partly because our culture has forced females to be identified with many of these characteristics.

The authoritarian and sedentary classroom atmosphere that prevails in some schools and that involves the "sit still and listen" syndrome, fails to take into account the greater activity drive and physical aggressiveness of boys. What have been characterized as feminization traits prevailing in many elementary schools tend to have an adverse influence on the young male child as far as learning is concerned.

Some studies have shown that as far as hyperactivity is concerned, boys may outnumber girls by a ratio of as much as nine to one. This may be one of the reasons why teachers generally tend to rate young males as being so much more aggressive than females with the result that young boys are considered to be more negative and extroverted. Because of these characteristics, boys generally have poorer relationships with their teachers than do girls, and in the area of behavior problems and discipline in the age range from five to eight years, boys account for twice as many disturbances as girls. The importance of this factor is borne out when it is considered that good teacher-pupil relationships tend to raise the achievement levels of both sexes.

Various studies have shown that girls generally receive higher grades than boys although boys may achieve as well as and in some instances better than, girls. It is also clearly evident that boys in the early years fail twice as often as girls even when there is no significant difference between intelligence and achievement test scores of both sexes. This suggests that even though both sexes have the same intellectual tools, there are other factors that are against learning as far as boys are concerned.

If one is willing to accept the research findings and observational evidence appearing in the child development literature regarding the premise outlined here, then the question is: "What attempts, if any, are being made to improve the condition?" At one time it was thought that the solution might lie in defeminization of the schools at the early age levels by putting more men into classrooms. This apparently has met with little success because the learning environment remains essentially the same regardless of the sex of the teacher. Some educators have suggested that little boys start school later or that little girls start earlier. The problem with this, of course, is that state laws concerned with school entrance are likely to distinguish only in terms of age and not sex. In a few remote instances some schools have experimented with separating boys and girls at the early grade levels. In some cases this form of grouping has resulted in both groups achieving at a higher level than when the sexes were in classes together.

The major question that must be posed is: "What *can* be done to at least partially restructure an environment that will be more favorable to the learning of young boys?" One step in this direction recommended by various child development specialists is to develop curriculum content that is more *action* oriented, thus taking into account the basic need for motor activity involved in human movement. This is to say that deep consideration might well be given to learning activities through which excess energy, especially of boys, can be utilized. The extent to which this kind of curriculum content would make learning less stressful for boys is not entirely known; however, experimentation by the present authors shows definite possibilities along these lines. (NOTE: For a detailed account of this approach the reader is referred to: Humphrey, James H., and Humphrey, Joy N.: *Help Your Child Learn the 3R's Through Active Play*. Springfield, IL, Charles C Thomas, Publisher, 1980.)

SOME GENERAL PRINCIPLES TO APPLY IN DEALING WITH STRESS

Obviously, there are no resolute standard procedures that are guaranteed to relieve a person entirely from undesirable stress. There are, however, certain general principles that may be applied to help alleviate stressful conditions.

All life pursuits involve both *general* and *specific* factors. In the case of dealing with stress, there are certain general principles that are likely to apply to most individuals. There are certain specific procedures for coping with stress that may be used by an individual in terms of how these procedures might meet his or her particular needs. The present discussion is concerned with some general principles of dealing with stress that in one way or another can be applied to practically all teachers, parents, *and* children.

We interpret the term *principle* to mean *guide to action*. Thus, the following general principles for dealing with stress should be considered as guidelines, but not necessarily in any particular order of importance. Moreover, it should be recognized that each principle is not a separate entity unto itself. This means that all of the principles are in some way interrelated and interdependent upon each other.

    1. *Personal health practice should be carefully observed.* This is an easy principle to accept, but sometimes it is a difficult one to implement. No one is against health,

but not everyone abides by those practices which can help to maintain a suitable level of health. Teachers with their imposing schedules may be prone to neglect the basic requirements that are essential for the human organism to reach an adequate functional level. Disregard for important needs such as proper diet, adequate sleep and rest, sufficient physical activity, and balancing work with play can reduce one's ability to cope with the stressful conditions inherent in the job of teaching.

Parents should accept the major share of the responsibility for health practices of their children, thus, at least partially eliminating unacceptable health behaviors that would be stress inducing for children.

2. *There should be continuous self-evaluation.* The practice of constantly taking stock on one's activities can help to minimize problems encountered on the job. This can be accomplished in part by taking a little time at the end of each day for an evaluation of the events that occurred during the day and reactions to those events. Setting aside this time period to review performance in the classroom is not only important to the achievement of goals, but it is also important for remaining objective. Teachers will more likely be able to identify certain problems over which they have no control, and thus, they will try to make an adjustment until such time that a positive change can be affected. Parents should consider this same practice and attempt to guide their children in a similar direction.

3. *Learn to recognize your own accomplishments.* One must learn to recognize his own accomplishments and praise himself for them, especially if such praise is not offered by others. This is generally known as "stroking" or "patting one's self on the back," so to speak. In practicing this procedure teachers can develop positive attitudes and/or belief systems about their own accomplishments and thus reduce stress. The same can be said for parents as they try to instill this idea into the lives of their children.

4. *Learn to take one thing at a time.* This is concerned with time budgeting and procrastination. Teachers, parents, and children are likely to put things off, and as a consequence, frustrations can build up as tasks pile up. There is a need to sort out those tasks in order of importance and attack them one at a time. Proper budgeting of time can help to alleviate procrastination, which in itself can be a stress inducing factor. Budgeting of time can help to eliminate worries of time urgency and the feeling of "too much to do in too short a time."
5. *Learn to take things less seriously.* This should not be interpreted to mean that teaching and parenting should not be taken seriously. It does mean that there can be a fine line between what is actually serious and what is not. Sometimes when people look back at a particular event, they may wonder how they could have become so excited about it. Those teachers who are able to see the humorous side in the classroom tend to look at a potentially stressful situation more objectively, and this can assist in keeping stress levels low.
6. *Do things for others.* Teachers and parents can sometimes take their minds off their own stressful conditions by offering to do something for other persons. Children should be taught to develop this concept early in life. When individuals are helpful to others in attempting to relieve them of stress, they in turn will tend to be relieved of stress themselves. Much research tends to show that those persons who volunteer to help others often times get as much benefit from this practice as those they volunteer to help. In this regard, it has been clearly demonstrated that older children who have reading problems improve in their own reading ability when they assist younger children with these same problems.
7. *Talk things over with others.* Teachers and parents sometimes tend to keep things to themselves; hence, they may not be aware that others may be disturbed by the same things. Sometimes discussing something with a colleague or with a spouse can help one see things in a much different light. It is important to keep in mind

that such discussion should be positive and objective lest it degenerate into idle gossip. This, of course, can tend to cause deterioration of a situation that is already at a low ebb.

8. *Stress should not be confused with challenge.* Often teachers relate stress to producing tensions and therefore expect anxiety to result. Contrary to this, constructive stress in the right amounts can challenge a teacher and promote motivation, thinking, and task completion. Thus, recognizing stress as a natural phenomenon of life is no doubt one of the first and most important steps in dealing with it. This is a concept that we should make every effort to develop with children at an early age.

Chapter 4

RELAXATION AND STRESS REDUCTION

MOST of us, teachers, parents, and children, need some type of relaxation in order to relieve the tensions encountered in daily living. The purpose of this chapter is to explore various facets of relaxation along with those kinds of conditions which tend to produce a relaxed state. Emphasis will be placed on procedures that teachers and parents can use for relaxation along with ways of teaching children about this means of reducing stress.

THE MEANING OF RELAXATION

The reality of muscle fibers is that they have a response repertoire of one. All they can do is contract and this is the response they make to the electrochemical stimulation of impulses carried via the motor nerves. *Relaxation* is the removal of this stimulation.[1]

A relatively new term *relaxation response* has been coined by Dr. Herbert Benson.[2] This involves a number of bodily changes that occur in the organism when one experiences deep muscle relaxation. There is a response against "overstress" which brings on these bodily changes and brings the body back into what is a healthier balance. Thus, the purpose of any kind of relaxation

---

[1] Brown, Barbara B.: *Stress and the Art of Biofeedback.* New York, Bantam Books, Inc., 1978, p. 31.

[2] Benson, Herbert: *The Relaxation Response.* New York, William Morrow and Company, Inc., 1975, p. 18.

technique should be to induce a relaxation response.

From the point of view of the physiologist, relaxation is sometimes considered as "zero activity," or as nearly zero as one can manage in the neuromuscular system. That is, it is a neuromuscular accomplishment that results in a reduction, or possible complete absence of muscle tone in a part of the body on in the entire body. It has been suggested that a primary value of relaxation lies in the lowering of brain and spinal cord activity, resulting from a reduction of nerve impulses arising in muscle spindles and other sense endings in muscles, tendons, and joins structures.

The terms *relaxation, refreshment,* and *recreation* are often confused in their meaning. While all of these factors are important to the well-being of the human organism, they should not be used interchangeably to mean the same thing. *Refreshment* is the result of an improved blood supply to the brain for "refreshment" from central fatigue and to the muscles for the disposition of their waste products. This explains in part why mild muscular activity is good for overcoming the fatigue of sitting quietly (seventh inning stretch) and for hastening recovery after strenuous exercise (an athlete continuing running for a short distance slowly after a race.)

Recreation may be described as the experience from which a person emerges with the feeling of being "re-created." No single activity is sure to bring this experience to all members of a group nor is there assurance that an activity will provide recreation again for a given person because it did so the last time. These are more the marks of a psychological than a physiological experience. An important essential requirement for a recreational activity is that it completely engross the individual, that is, it must engage his or her entire undivided attention. It is really escape from the disintegrating effects of distraction to the healing effect of totally integrated activity. Experiences that produce this effect may range from a hard game of tennis to the reading of a comic strip.[3]

Some individuals consider recreation and relaxation to be one and the same thing, which is *not* the case. Recreation can be considered a type of mental diversion that can be helpful in relieving tenson. While mental and muscular tension are interrelated, it is

---

[3] Steinhaus, Arthur: *Toward an Understanding of Health and Physical Education.* Dubuque, IA, Wm. C. Brown Publishers, 1963, p. 322.

in the muscle that the tension state is manifested.

For many years recommendations have been made as regards procedures individuals might apply in an effort to relax. Examples of some of these procedures are submitted in the ensuing discussions. In consideration of any technique that is designed to accomplish relaxation, one very important factor that needs to be taken into account is that learning to relax is a skill. That is, it is a skill based on the kinesthetic awareness of feelings of *tonus* (the normal degree of contraction present in most muscles that keeps them always ready to function when needed). Unfortunately, it is a skill that very few of us use and practice — probably because we have little awareness of how to go about it.

One of the first steps in learning to relax is to experience tension. That is, one should be sensitive to tensions that exist in his or her body. This can be accomplished by voluntarily contracting a given muscle group, first very strongly and then, less and less. Emphasis should be placed on detecting the signal of tension as the first step in "letting go" (relaxing).

As in the case of any muscular skill, learning how to relax takes time, and one should not expect to achieve complete satisfaction immediately. After one has identified a relaxation technique with which he or she feels comfortable, increased practice should eventually achieve satisfactory results.

PROGRESSIVE RELAXATION

The technique of progressive relaxation was developed by Dr. Edmund Jacobson over a half century ago. It is still the technique most often referred to in the literature and probably the one that has had the most widespread application. (Yet, our studies as reported on the subject revealed that only one percent of teachers surveyed used this technique.)[4] In this technique the person concentrates on progressively relaxing one muscle group after another. The technique is based on the procedure of comparing the difference between tension and relaxation. That is, as previously mentioned, one senses the feeling of tension in order to get the feeling of relaxation.

---

[4] Humphrey, James H., and Humphrey, Joy N.: *How Teachers Can Cope With Stress*, College Park, MD, James H. Humphrey and Joy N. Humphrey, 1980, p. 48.

You might wish to try the traditional experiment used to demonstrate this phenomenon. Raise one arm so that the palm of the hand is facing outward away from your face. Now, bend the wrist backward, and try to point the fingers back toward your face and down toward the forearm. You should feel some *strain* at the wrist joint. You should also feel something else in the muscle, and this is tension, which is due to the muscle contracting the hand backward. Now, flop the hand forward with the fingers pointing downward, and you will have accomplished a *tension - relaxation* cycle

As mentioned previously, learning to relax is a skill that you can develop in applying the principles of progressive relaxation. One of the first steps is to be able to identify the various muscle groups and how to tense them so that tension and relaxation can be experienced. Before we make suggestions on how to tense and relax the various muscles there are certain other preliminary measures that need to be taken into account, as follow:

1. You must understand that this procedure takes time, and like anything else, the more you practice, the more proficient you should become with the skill.
2. Progressive relaxation is not the kind of thing to be done spontaneously, and you should be prepared to spend from twenty to thirty minutes daily in tensing-relaxing activities.
3. The particular time of day is important, and this is pretty much an individual matter. Some recommendations suggest that progressive relaxation be practiced daily, sometime during the day and again in the evening before retiring. For teachers this would be difficult unless one time period was set aside before going to school in the morning. This might be a good possibility and might help a teacher to start the day relaxed.
4. It is important to find a suitable place to practice the tensing-relaxing activities. Again, this is an individual matter with some preferring a bed or couch and others a comfortable chair.
5. Consideration should be given to the amount of time a given muscle is tensed. You should be sure that you are able to feel the difference between tension and relaxa-

tion. This means that tension should be maintained from about four to not more than eight seconds.
6. Another important point is to take into account what sort of "mental practice," if any, should be used as the muscles are tensed and relaxed. In this connection, some clinical psychologists may use mental practice predominantly, as in the case of the use of imagery suggested later in the chapter.
7. Breathing is an important concomitant in tensing and relaxing muscles. To begin, it is suggested that three or more deep breaths be taken and held for about five seconds. This will tend to make a better rhythm in breathing. Controlled breathing makes it easier to relax, and it is most effective when it is done deeply and slowly. It is ordinarily recommended that one should inhale deeply when the muscles are tensed and exhale slowly when "letting go."

How to Tense and Relax Various Muscles

Muscle groups may be identified in different ways. The classification given here consists of four different groups: (1) muscles of the head, face, tongue, and neck, (2) muscles of the trunk, (3) muscles of the upper extremities, and (4) muscles of the lower extremities.

Muscles of the Head, Face, Tongue, and Neck

There are two chief muscles of the head, the one covering the back of the head, and the one covering the front of the skull. There are about thirty muscles of the face including muscles of the orbit and eyelids, mastication, lips, tongue, and neck. Incidentally, it has been estimated that it takes twenty-six facial muscles to frown and a proportionately much smaller number to smile.

Muscles of this group may be tensed and relaxed as follows (relaxation is accomplished by "letting go" after tensing):
1. Raise your eyebrows by opening the eyes as wide as possible. You might wish to look into a mirror to see if you have formed wrinkles on the forehead.
2. Tense the muscles on either side of your nose like you were going to sneeze.

3. Dilate or flare out the nostrils.
4. Force an extended smile from "ear to ear" at the same time clenching your teeth.
5. Pull one corner of the mouth up and then the other up and out as in a "villainous sneer."
6. Draw your chin down as close to your chest as possible.
7. Do the opposite of the above trying to draw your head back as close to your back as possible.

Muscles of the Trunk

Included in this group are the muscles of the back, chest, abdomen and pelvis. The following are some ways you can tense some of these muscles:

1. Bring your chest forward, and at the same time put your shoulders back with emphasis on bringing your shoulder blades as close together as possible.
2. Try to round your shoulders and bring your shoulder blades far apart. This is pretty much the opposite of the above.
3. Give your shoulders a shrug, trying to bring them up to your ears at the same time as you try to bring your neck downward.
4. Breathe deeply, hold it momentarily, and then blow out the air from your lungs rapidly.
5. Draw in your stomach so that your chest is out beyond your stomach. Exert your stomach muscles by forcing out to make it look like you are fatter in that area than you are.

Muscles of the Upper Extremities

This group includes muscles of the hands, forearms, upper arms, and shoulders. A number of muscles situated in the trunk may be grouped with the muscles of the upper extremities, their function being to attach the upper limbs to the trunk and move the shoulders and arms. In view of this, there is some overlapping in muscle groups *two* and *three*. Following are some ways to tense some of these muscles:

1. Clench the fist, and then open the hand extending the fingers as far as possible.

2. Raise one arm shoulder high and parallel to the floor. Bend at the elbow, and bring the hand in toward the shoulder. Try to touch your shoulder while attempting to move the shoulder away from the hand. Flex your opposite biceps in the same manner.
3. Stretch one arm out to the side of the body, and try to point the fingers backward toward the body. Do the same with the other arm.
4. Hold the arm out the same way as above, but this time have the palm facing up, and point the fingers inward toward the body. Do the same with the other arm.
5. Stretch one arm out to the side, clench the fist, and roll the wrist around slowly. Do the same with the other arm.

Muscles of the Lower Extremities

This group includes muscles of the hips, thighs, legs, feet, and buttocks. Following are ways to tense some of these muscles:
1. Hold one leg out straight, and point your toes as far forward as you can. Do the same with the other leg.
2. Do the same as the above, but point your toes as far backward as you can.
3. Turn each foot outward as far as you can and release. Do just the opposite by turning the foot inward as far as you can.
4. Try to draw the thigh muscles up so that you can see the form of the muscles.
5. Make your buttocks tense by pushing down if you are sitting in a chair. If you are lying down, try to draw the muscles of the buttocks in close by attempting to force the cheeks together.

The above suggestions include several possibilities for tensing various muscles of the body. As you practice some of these, you will also discover other ways to tense and then let go. A word of caution, in the early stages you should be alert to the possibility of cramping certain muscles. This can happen particularly with those muscles that are not frequently used. This means that at the beginning you should proceed carefully. It might be a good idea to keep a record or diary of your sessions so that you can refer back to these experiences if this might be necessary. This will also help you get into each new session by reviewing your experiences in previous sessions.

USE OF MENTAL PRACTICE AND IMAGERY IN RELAXATION

We have previously mentioned that a person might want to take into account the use of *mental practice* and *imagery* in producing a relaxed state. Mental practice has been described as the "symbolic rehearsal of a physical activity in the absence of any gross muscular movement."[5] This means that a person imagines in his own mind the way he will perform a given activity. Imagery is concerned with the development of a mental image that may aid one in the performance of an activity. In mental practice the person is likely to think through on his own what he is going to do. With imagery another person (teacher) may suggest a condition, and the performer then tries to effect a mental image of the condition. (As we shall see later in the chapter a form of imagery plays an important part in *creative relaxation*.)

The use of mental practice in performing motor skills is not new. Research in this general area has been going on for half a century. This research has revealed that imagining a movement will likely produce recordable electric action potentials emanating from the muscle groups that would be called up if the movement were to be actually carried out. In addition, most mental activity is accompanied by general rises in muscular tension.[6]

One procedure in the use of mental practice for relaxation is that of making suggestions to one's self. For the most part, as children, we first learn to act on the basis of verbal instructions from others. Later, we learn to guide and direct our own behavior on the basis of our own language activities—we literally talk to ourselves, giving ourselves instructions. This point of view has long been supported by research[7] and postulates that speech as a form

---

[5] Whiting, H. T. A.: *Acquiring Ball Skills*. Philadelphia, Lea & Febiger, 1969, p. 82.

---

[6] Cratty, Bryant J.: *Physical Expressions of Intelligence*. Englewood Cliffs, NJ, Prentice-Hall, Inc., 1972, p. 144-145.

---

[7] Luria, A. R.: Development of the directive function of speech in early childhood. *Word*, 1959.

of communication between children and adults later becomes a means of organizing the child's own behavior. That is, the function that was previously divided between two people—child and adult—becomes an internal function of human behavior.

An example is an approach recommended by Dr. C. Eugene Walker involving one making relaxation-connected statements to himself or herself. He suggests the following specific illustration:

> I am going to relax completely. First, I will relax my forehead and scalp. I will let all the muscles of my forehead and scalp relax and become completely at rest. All of the wrinkles will come out of my forehead and that part of my body will relax completely. Now, I will relax the muscles of my face. I will just let them relax and go limp. There will be no tension in my jaw. Next, I will relax my neck muscles. Just let them become tranquil and allow all the pressure to leave them. My neck muscles are relaxing completely. Now, I will relax the muscles of my shoulders. That relaxation will spread down my arms to the elbows, down the forearm to wrists, hands, and fingers. My arms will just dangle from the frame of my body. I will now relax the muscles of my chest. I will let them relax. I will take a deep breath and relax, letting all the tightness and tenseness leave. My breathing will now be normal and relaxed, and I will relax the muscles of my stomach. Now I will relax all of the muscles up and down both sides of the spine; now the waist, buttocks, and thighs down to my knees. Now the relaxation will spread to the calves of my legs, ankles, feet, and toes. I will just lie here and continue to let all of the muscles go completely limp. I will become completely relaxed from the top of my head to the tips of my toes.[8]

A number of researchers report success in using imagery as an aspect of relaxation with children. Kanfer and Goldstein[9] used imagery to advantage in their work on self-instructional training with hyperactive and impulsive children. Schneider and Robin[10]

---

[8] Walker, C. Eugene: *Learn to Relax, 13 Ways to Reduce Tension,* Englewood Cliffs, NJ, Prentice-Hall, Inc., 1975, p. 10.

[9] Kanfer, F., and Goldstein, A. P.: *Helping People Change: A Textbook of Methods,* New York, The Pergamon Press, 1975.

[10] Schneider, M., and Robin, A.: *Turtle Manual.* Stony Brook, NY, Psychology Department, State University of New York, 1974.

had success with imagery in the development of a self-control program. They developed the technique of training disruptive children to have impulse control by pairing imagery and relaxation.

In what he termed the "release only" phase of relaxation training, McBrien[11] used instructions involving imagery as follows:

> Just imagine you are lying on your back on soft green grass ...you are so comfortable as you look up through the branches and leaves of a shade tree at the deep blue sky... you can see soft white puffy clouds floating by. (Further instructions to focus on the pleasant feeling of relaxation would then follow.)

Another way imagery can be used to promote a relaxed state is by making short *comparative* statements to children such as "float like a feather" or "melt like ice." The creative adult and child will be able to think up many such comparative statements to assist in producing a relaxed state.

TEACHERS CAN REDUCE CLASSROOM STRESS THROUGH ISOMETRIC RELAXATION

It is the purpose of this section of the chapter to explore the place of *physical activity* and *exercise* as a "relaxative" in coping with stress. More specifically we will recommend certain "relaxation exercises" that a teacher can engage in when conditions become stressful in the classroom.

Physical Activity and Exercise

When used in connection with the human organism, the term *physical* means a concern for the body and its needs. The term *activity* derives from the word *active*, one meaning of which is the requirement of action. Thus, when the two words *physical* and *activity* are used together, it implies body action. This is a broad term and could include any voluntary and/or involuntary body movement. When such body movement is practiced for the purpose of developing and maintaining physical fitness, it is ordinarily referred to as physical *exercise*. What we are primarily concerned with here are the broad area of physical activity and the more specific area of physical exercise as they relate to stress.

---

[11]McBrien, Robert J.: Using relaxation methods with first grade boys. *Elementary School Guidance and Counseling,* February, 1978.

The answer to the question, "Why exercise?" is relatively simple. Wherever there is muscle, there is a need for movement. The human body contains more than 600 muscles. Muscles make possible every overt motion. They also push food along the digestive tract, suck air into the lungs, and tighten blood vessels to raise blood pressure when more pressure is needed to meet an emergency. The heart itself is a muscular pump. Muscles are meant to be used and when they are not used, or not used enough, they can deteriorate. If we are habitually inactive, we succumb to the philosophy of easy living; we must then pay the price in decreased efficiency.

Importance of Physical Exercise in Coping with Stress

The value of exercise as a means of coping with stress is well documented by various sources. According to McQuade and Aikman,[12] one of the many stresses we suffer from is from the stress of our own pent-up aggressive drives. When we express these drives in physical action, we are better off: further, that exercise not only dispels one form of stress in our lives, but it also enables us to bear up better against stress in general.

Similarly, Jencks[13] reports that physical and emotional trauma upset the balance of body and mind, so that much energy is wasted in muscular tension, bringing on unnecessary tiredness and exhaustion. If stress reactions become habit patterns, the muscles and tendons shorten and thicken, and excessive connective tissue is deposited, causing a general consolidation of tissues. She comments further that excess energy, released by action of the sympathetic nervous system, if not immediately dissipated by muscular action, produces muscular or nervous tension and this tension may then be dissipated by muscular action in the form of exercise.

Relaxation Exercises to Cope with Stress in the Classroom

The foregoing discussion has focused on the importance of physical activity in helping one cope with stress. The present dis-

---

[12] McQuade, Walter and Aikman, Ann: *Stress.* New York, E. P. Dutton & Co., Inc., 1974, p. 130.

[13] Jencks, Beata: *Your Body, Biofeedback at Its Best.* Chicago, Nelson-Hall, Inc., 1977, p. 151, 172.

cussion is concerned with a teacher's active behavior in a stressful situation. More specifically, what can a teacher do in the way of physical activity (and at the same time effect a relaxed state) to cope with a stressful situation arising in the classroom?

Various authentic pronouncements have been made that support the idea that instant activity can be beneficial. For example, Gal and Lazarus[14] report that being engaged in activity—rather than remaining passive—is preferable for most individuals in most stressful situations and can be highly effective in reducing threat and distress. Lazarus[15] has also maintained that a person may alter his or her psychological and physiological stress reactions in a given situation simply by taking action and this in turn will affect his or her appraisal of the situation thereby ultimately altering the stress reaction.

Before continuing with our specific recommendations for classroom "relaxation isometrics" designed to cope with stressful situations, it seems important to mention the two kinds of strength involved in exercise. These are *isometric* strength and *isotonic* strength. Isometric strength involves the maximal amount of force that can be applied against a fixed resistance during one all out effort. An example of this is pushing or pulling against an object. Isotonic strength involves the amount of resistance one can overcome during one application of force through the full range of motion in a given joint or joints. An example of this would be picking up a weight and flexing the elbows while lifting the weight, let us say to shoulder height.

What then are some of the "relaxation isometrics" that a teacher can engage in as reactions to a stressful situation in the classroom? Obviously, it would not be appropriate to drop to the floor and start doing pushups or to break into a two-mile jog around the room. The isometrics that we are recommending can be performed in a more or less subtle manner and not even be noticed by students or other observers. Moreover, they follow the tensing-releasing procedure in progressive relaxation discussed

---

[14]Gal, Reuven and Lazarus, Richard S.: The role of activity in anticipating and confronting stressful situations.*Journal of Human Stress,* December, 1975.

---

[15]Lazarus, Richard S.: The self-regulation of emotion. In Levy, L. (Ed.) *Parameters of Emotion.* New York, Raven Press, 1975.

earlier in the chapter. The following are some possibilities, and certainly creative teachers will be able to think of numerous others. (Remember, relaxation is accomplished by "letting go" after about four to eight seconds.)

1. *Hand and Head Press.* Interweave fingers and place hands at the back of the head with elbows pointing out. Push the head backward on the hands while simultaneously pulling the head forward with the hands. Although this can be done while standing, it can also be done while sitting at the desk and is less conspicuous.

2. *Wall Press.* Stand with the back against the wall. Allow the arms to hang down at the sides. Turn the hands toward the wall and press the wall with the palms, keeping the arms straight.

3. *Hand Pull.* Bend the right elbow and bring the right hand in with the palm up close to the front of the body. Put the left hand in the right hand. Try to curl the right arm upward while simultaneously resisting with the left hand. Repeat, using the opposite pressure. This can be done while standing or while sitting at the desk.

4. *Hand Push.* The hands are clasped with the palms together close to the chest with the elbows pointing out. Press the hands together firmly. This can be done while standing or while sitting at the desk.

5. *Leg Press.* While sitting at the desk, cross the left ankle over the right ankle. The feet are on the floor, and the legs are at about a right angle. Try to straighten the right leg, while resisting with the left leg. Repeat, with the right ankle over the left ankle.

6. *The Gripper.* Place one hand in the other hand and grip hard. This can be done while standing or sitting at the desk. Another variation is to grip an object. While standing, this could be the arms of a chair or the seat.

7. *Chair Push.* While sitting at the desk with the hands on the arm rest of the chair, push down with the hands. The entire buttocks can be raised from the chair seat.

One or both feet can be lifted off the floor, or both feet can remain in contact with the floor.

8. *Hip Lifter.* While sitting at the desk, lift one buttock after the other from the chair seat. Try to keep the head from moving. The hands can be placed at the sides of the chair seat for balance.

9. *Heel and Toe.* From a standing position, rise on the toes. Come back down on the heels while raising both the toes and the balls of the feet.

10. *Fist Clencher.* Clench the fist and then open the hands extending the fingers.

This short list is comprised of representative examples of "relaxation isometric" exercises, and they are actually referred to by some people as *stress* exercises. We should mention that the exercises recommended above have met with success in producing a relaxed state for many teachers who have practiced them when distressing situations arise in the classroom.

USING RELAXATION WITH CHILDREN

Up to this point, with a few minor exceptions, our discussions in this chapter have been concerned with providing an understanding about relaxation for adults (teachers and parents). We now turn our attention to the matter of how teachers and parents can convey information about the phenomenon of relaxation to children, as well as how this procedure can be used as a basis for stress reduction in children.

Until relatively recent years, the use of relaxation as a means of stress reduction appeared to be used primarily with adults; however, in more modern times relaxation procedures have been found to be very useful with children. Moreover, there is some objective evidence to support the idea that the practice of relaxation with children can be beneficial for them in various ways. For example, one study found that there could be significant changes in attentiveness of school children when relaxation training was used.[16] Other studies have shown that various measures of anxiety can be

---

[16]Bednarova, N., An investigation concerning the influence of psychotonic exercises upon the indices of concentration of attentiveness. *Teor. Prax. Telex. Vychov.*, 16, 1968.

lowered as a result of the use of relaxation procedures.[17,18] It has also been found that there is improvement of self-help skills of retarded children after using relaxation exercises accompanied by music.[19]

Formats of Relaxation Training Programs for Children

There are a variety of different formats that can be used as a means of providing satisfactory relaxation training for children. Two such formats are discussed here.

Game Format

An example of the successful use of the game format is that that is suggested by McBrien.[20] He used this approach in the tensing and releasing phase with the game Simon Says. Each muscle group to be tensed and then relaxed was prefaced by "Simon says," that is, "Simon says to close your eyes...Simon says to make your eyebrows touch your hair...Simon says to let go and feel your eyes relax." A five second tensing of any muscle was followed by fifteen seconds of releasing the muscle. The sequence for relaxing the muscles prefaced by "Simon says" was as follows:

1. Head
    a. Try to make your eyebrows touch your hair.
    b. Squeeze your eyes shut.
    c. Wrinkle up your nose.
    d. Press your lips together.
    e. Press your tongue against the roof of your mouth.
2. Shoulders and back
    a. Lift your shoulders, and try to touch your ears.
    b. Bring your shoulders back as far as they will go.

---

[17] Johnson, D. I., and Spielberger, C. D.: The effects of relaxation training and the passage of time on measures of static and trait anxiety. *J Clin Psychol,* 1968.

---

[18] Keat, D. B.: Broad spectrum behavior therapy with children: A case presentation. *Behavior Therapy,* 3, 1972.

---

[19] Cratty, Bryant J.: *Physical Expressions of Intelligence.* Englewood Cliffs, NJ, Prentice-Hall, Inc., 1972, p. 183.

---

[20] McBrien, Robert J.: Using relaxation methods with first-grade boys. *Elementary School Guidance and Counseling,* February, 1978.

3. Hands and arms
   a. Make your fist as tight as you can.
   b. Show me your arm muscles.
4. Stomach—Make your stomach as hard as you can; pull it way in.
5. Upper legs
   a. Lift your legs and feet off the floor.
   b. Press your knees together.
6. Lower legs and feet
   a. Press your ankles together.
   b. Press your feet together against the floor.

Note: The game Simon Says is played as follows: One or more children face the person who plays Simon. Every time Simon says to do something: the children do it; however, if a command is given without the prefix "Simon says," the children remain motionless. For example, when the leader issues the command "Simon says press your ankles together," everyone does this, but if the person playing Simon says, "Press your knees together," the children do not execute the command.

Guided Progressive Format

This format was used successfully by Krampf, Hopkins, and Byrd as a part of a Summer Youth Fitness School for children ages seven to fourteen.[21] There was a series of *guided progressive sessions* used to assist the participants in becoming aware of their tensions and how to release these tensions. In this format there are four component parts: (1) relaxation of individual muscles, (2) relaxation of group muscles, (3) relaxation of principal muscle groups, and (4) relaxation of the total body.

It is suggested that the practice setting be conducive to relaxation, and this includes a comfortable room temperature, loose-fitting clothing, lighting that is not too bright, and the provision of a soft surface such as mats. The first step involves practice of controlled breathing followed by helping children to realize the difference between being tense and limp. The next step is to use the tensing-releasing procedure, progressing through the various

---

[21] Krampf, Harry, Hopkins, Dave, and Bird, John: Muscular relaxation for the elementary student. *Journal of Physical Education and Recreation,* April, 1979.

body parts.

CREATIVE RELAXATION

As indicated by the title, the use of creative relaxation as a stress reduction technique with children is a major function of this book. (To the best of our present knowledge, the term "creative relaxation" originated with the present authors.)

Creative relaxation combines a form of imagery and tensing and releasing. A child or a group of children with various degrees of adult guidance creates a movement(s) designed to tense and relax individual muscles, muscle groups, or the entire body. When this involves an individual muscle or a group of muscles, it can be called specific relaxation, and when it involves the entire body, it can be referred to as general relaxation. The procedure is applicable in the home to be used by the parent, as well as applicable in the school setting to be used by the teacher. When used with one child or several children, the procedures are essentially the same.

Creative relaxation simply means that there are contrasting creative movements that give the effect of tensing and letting go. The two final chapters are devoted to providing a large number of creative movements for use in creative relaxation. Nevertheless an illustration is provided here for a better understanding of the concept at this point.

This example shows the contrast (tensing and letting go) of the muscles in an upper extremity (arm). The teacher or parent could start by raising a question, such as "What would you say is the main difference between a ball bat and a jump rope?" This question is then discussed with the children and will no doubt lead to the major difference being that a ball bat is hard and stiff and that a jump rope is soft and limp. The teacher or parent might then proceed as follows:

> Let's see if we can all make one of our arms be like a ball bat." (children create this movement). "Now quickly, can you make your arm be like a jump rope?" (children create the movement by releasing the tensed arm.)

The experience can then be evaluated by using questions such as: "How did your arm feel when you made it like a bat?" and "How did your arm feel when you made it like a jump rope?"

The creative adult along with the children can produce a discussion that will increase an understanding of the relaxation phenomenon. This is but one approach, and adults are limited only by their own creativity and imagination.

Chapter 5

CREATIVE MOVEMENT

IN order to provide the reader with an understanding of the meaning of this chapter title, it seems appropriate at the outset to provide a literal description of *creative movement*. The English word *creative* derives from the French word *createn* and the Latin word *creatus* both of which mean "to bring into existence." The term *movement*, when applied to the human organism, simply means a "change in body position." Therefore, when we put the two words *creative* and *movement* together, the interpretation is bringing something into existence or being creative by expressing one's self by means of body movement. This creative action can pertain to the whole body or various body parts, and as mentioned previously, this procedure is basic to creative relaxation as a means of stress reduction in children.

One of the utmost concerns to educators in our modern democratic society is the problem of how to provide for creative expression so that a child may develop to the fullest extent of his potentialities. Democracy is only beginning to understand the power of the individual as perhaps the most dynamic force in the world today. It is in this frame of reference that creativity should come clearly into focus, because many of the problems in our complex society can be solved mainly through creative thinking.

Creative experience involves *self*-expression. It is concerned with the need to experiment, to express original ideas, and to think. Creativity and childhood enjoy a congruous relationship because children are naturally creative. They imagine. They pretend.

Creative Movement 81

They are uninhibited. They are not only original, but actually ingenious in their thoughts and actions. Indeed, creativity is a characteristic inherent in the lives of practically all children. It may range from some children who create as a natural form of expression without adult stimulation to others who may need varying degrees of adult guidance and encouragement.

There are a variety of media for creative expression (art, music, and writing) that are considered the traditional approaches to creative expression; however, the very essence of creative expression is movement. Movement, as a form of creativity, uses the body as the instrument of expression. For the young child, the most natural form of creative expression is movement. Because of their very nature, children have a natural inclination for movement, and they use this medium as the basic form of creative expression. Movement is the child's universal language, a most important form of communication, and a most meaningful way of learning.

The possibilities of creative movement as a medium for learning are almost endless. A specific example is the work of the present authors in using creative movement as a procedure in helping children to learn to read and to improve upon their ability to read once they have learned to do so.

(Note: A brief overview of this procedure is presented here. For a more detailed account the reader is referred to: Humphrey, James H. and Humphrey, Joy N.: *Help Your Child Learn the 3 R's Through Active Play.* Springfield, Illinois, Charles C Thomas, Publisher, 1980.)

Our procedure for learning to read through the use of active play (creative movement) is identified as the *APAV Technique,* an example of which will be presented later. The APAV Technique involves a learning sequence of *auditory input* to *play* (creative movement) to *auditory-visual input,* as depicted in the following diagram.

*A*uditory   Play   *A*uditory-*V*isual
                         (creative movement)

Essentially, this technique is a procedure for working through creative movement experiences in active play to develop comprehension first in listening and then in reading. The A→P aspect of APAV is a directed listening-thinking activity. The child first receives the thoughts and feelings expressed in an active play story through the auditory sense by listening to the story read by the teacher or parent. Following this, the child engages in the active play experiences that are inherent in the story. He demonstrates his understanding of and reaction to the story through creative movements. By engaging in this creative experience, the development of comprehension becomes a part of the child's physical reality.

After the active play experience in the directed listening-thinking activity, the child moves to the final aspect of the APAV Technique (A-V), a combination of auditory and visual experience by listening to the story read by the teacher or parent and *reading along* with the teacher or parent. In this manner, comprehension is brought to the reading experience.

Although the sequence of listening to reading is a natural one, bridging the gap to the point of handling the verbal symbols required in reading poses various problems for many children. One of the outstanding features of the APAV Technique is that the creative movement involved in the active play experience helps to serve as a bridge between listening and reading by providing direct purposeful experience for the child through active play after listening to the story.

Following is an example of a story that the reader can use in applying the APAV Technique. Remember, first you read the story to the child; then with various degrees of guidance in creative movement he participates in the active play experience, and then you and the child read the story together.

The Funny Clown

I am a funny clown.
I move like a funny clown.
I jump.
I skip.
I run.
I stop.
I have fun.

This technique may be used with school age children who are encountering some difficulty with comprehension, and it can be used with the immediate preschool child to help him gain some sight words and develop listening skills. As far as the latter is concerned, we have had very successful experience with four- to five-year-old children, finding that many of them can retain what they have heard for a minimum of one week and sometimes even much longer. It has proved to be an outstanding way to use creative movement as a procedure for helping children learn.

APPROACHES TO THE USE OF CREATIVE MOVEMENT

In general, there are two broad approaches to the use of creative movement. These can be arbitrarily identified as *individual interpretation* and *dramatization*. The essential difference between the two is in the degree of structuring of the activities. Individual interpretation has little, if any, structuring and involves children moving in the way that they feel like moving. That is, the ideas for movement are supposed to originate with the children. Dramatization centers around some sort of story, plan, or idea that can provide various kinds of clues for children.

In individual interpretation, some sort of rhythmical accompaniment is *required* because the children are supposed to move in a way that the accompaniment makes them feel like moving. In dramatization the use of accompaniment is *optional*, depending upon the person conducting the activity as well as the nature of the activity itself. Incidentally, when accompaniment is used, the movements are ordinarily referred to as creative *rhythms*.

Although there are various kinds of accompaniment for rhythms and dances used with children, in creative rhythms a percussion instrument such as a drum is employed most frequently. The drum is an instrument that is easy to learn to play, and the person furnishing the accompaniment can change the tempo as needed. Again, we repeat that accompaniment is required for individual interpretation and that with the dramatization approach to the use of creative movement it is optional.

Although it is an excellent experience to provide for children, because of its very nature, individual interpretation is not applicable for use with *creative relaxation*, at least as it is conceived here. The reason for this is that the children need some sort of verbal clues as far as the contrasting movements involving tensing and releasing are concerned. Hereafter, when we refer to creative movement, we will be thinking of it in terms of the dramatization approach. An example of the use of the approach seems appropriate at this point.

This approach can involve (1) a story or idea about which the children already know or something with which they are familiar, (2) a story made up by the teacher, or (3) a story started by the teacher and added to by the children. (NOTE: Hereafter in our discussions we will refer to the adult conducting the activity as the "teacher." This means that it could be the teacher in school or the parent-teacher at home.)

In using a familiar story such as "Jack and the Beanstalk," the children can act out the story to drum accompaniment provided by the teacher. Two examples of something that the children already know about are the activities Flower Garden and Snowman. In Flower Garden the children curl up on the floor, each representing a flower seed. To suitable accompaniment, the children use axial movements (rising, stretching, turning, and the like) to "grow" as a flower. They finally rise to a standing position with arms above the head. In Snowman the children stand in informal order about the area as snowmen in the bright shining sun. They do a variety of movements that depict snowmen melting as a result of the hot sun.

An example of a story made up by the teacher is shown in the following simulated teaching procedure in which a *parade* theme is used with drum accompaniment.

Teacher: Boys and girls, how many of you know what a parade is?
(Children respond)
Teacher: Good. How many of you have seen a parade?
(Children respond)
Teacher: That's fine; most of you have seen a parade. What kinds of parades are there?
(Children respond)
Teacher: On what days do we have parades?
(Children respond)
Teacher: You have given several examples, and now I would like to tell you a story about a Fourth of July parade. This is a story about children watching a parade. In the parade was a group of soldiers. They marched along to the sound of music and the beat of a drum. Would someone

Creative Movement 85

like to show us how they marched?
(One child demonstrates to the drum accompaniment provided by the teacher. The children then evaluate the good things the "marching soldier" did.)

Teacher: George, because you did such a good job, you can be the head soldier, and everyone will march along behind you.
(The teacher accompanies the marching soldiers on the drum for a period of time, and then they return to their original places.)

Teacher: The children enjoyed watching the soldiers so much and tried to keep pace with them. How could they do this?
(The teacher sounds several fast beats, and a child mentions that the children would have to run to keep up.)

Teacher: That's right, Jack, can you show us how?
(The child runs to the accompaniment, good points are evaluated, and then all the children run for a short period of time and then return to their places.)

Teacher: Now, boys and girls, something very interesting happened. (The teacher sounds several loud slow beats on the drum.)

Teacher: What do you think that could have been?
(Children give several suggestions such as a cannon, base drum, etc. If none of the children suggest that it was a giant taking big steps, the teacher continues.)

Teacher: Boys and girls, it was a giant taking great big, giant steps. (The teacher goes through the same procedure as with the marching soldiers and running children, and the children move around the activity area with big giant steps to the drum accompaniment, then go back to their original places. The teacher can continue with suggestions from the children or end the story at this point.)

All of the ideas for use of creative movement above are suggestive points of departure to be taken. The imaginative teacher along with the children can develop many such ideas along these lines. Our concern will be to orient the ideas to creative movement that will result in relaxation. A large number of suggestions for this will comprise the final two chapters of the book.

SOME PRINCIPLES OF LEARNING APPLIED TO CREATIVE MOVEMENT

There are various basic facts about the nature of human beings of which we are now more cognizant than we were in the past. Essentially, these facts involve some of the fundamental aspects of the learning process, which all good teaching should take into account. Older concepts of teaching methods were based largely upon the idea that the teacher was the sole authority in terms of what was best for children, and that children were expected to learn regardless of the conditions surrounding the learning situation. For the most part, modern teaching replaces the older concepts with methods that are based on certain accepted beliefs of educational psychology. Outgrowths of these beliefs emerge in the form of principles of learning. The following principles provide important guidelines for arranging learning experiences for children, and they suggest how desirable learning can take place when the principles are satisfactorily applied to the teaching of creative movement.

1. *The child's own purposeful goals should guide his learning activities.* For a desirable learning situation to prevail, teachers should consider certain features about purposeful goals that guide learning activities. Of utmost importance is that the goal must seem worthwhile to the child. This will involve factors such as interest, attention, and motivation. Fortunately, in creative movement activities these factors are "built-in" qualities. Thus, the teacher does not necessarily need to "arouse" the child with various kinds of motivating devices.
2. *The child should be given freedom to create his own responses in the situation he faces.* This principle indicates that *problem solving* is a very important way of human learning and that the child will learn mainly only through experience, either direct or indirect. This implies that the teacher should provide every opportunity for the child to use his own judgment in the various situations that arise in the creative movement experience.
3. *The child agrees to and acts upon the learnings that he considers of most value to him.* Children accept as most valuable those things which are of greatest interest to

them. This principle implies in part, then, that there should be a satisfactory balance between *needs* and *interests* of children in their creative movement experiences. Although it is of extreme importance to consider the needs of children in developing experiences, the teacher should keep in mind that their interest is needed if the most desirable learning is to take place.

4. *The child should be given the opportunity to share cooperatively in learning experiences with others under the guidance, but not the control, of the teacher.* The point that should be emphasized here is that, although learning may be an individual matter, it can take place well in a group. This is to say that children learn individually, but that socialization can be retained. This can be achieved even if there are only two members participating, the teacher and the child.

5. *The teacher should act as a guide who understands the child as a growing organism.* This principle indicates that the teacher should consider learning as an evolving process and not just as instant behavior. If the teacher is to regard his or her efforts in terms of guidance and direction of behavior that results in learning, wisdom must be displayed as to when to "step in and teach" and when to step aside and watch for further opportunities to guide and direct behavior. The application of this principle precludes an approach that is teacher dominated. In this regard, the teacher could be guided by the old saying that "children should learn by monkeying and not by aping."

It is quite likely that teachers will have good success in using the creative movements in the following chapters to reduce stress through creative relaxation if they attempt to apply these principles. The main reason for this is that their efforts in helping children learn through creative movement will be in line with those conditions under which learning takes place most effectively.

Chapter 6

CREATIVE MOVEMENTS FOR GENERAL RELAXATION

WE mentioned previously that general relaxation involves the entire body and that specific relaxation is concerned with an individual muscle or a group of muscles. (The reader may wish to refer to chapter 4 for an identification of the four classifications of muscle groups.)

Specific relaxation as used here should not be confused with what some persons call *differential* relaxation. Those who use this term generally consider it to be concerned with relaxing all muscles except those that are actually needed for the particular occupation at hand. Perhaps it should be mentioned that we use the terms *general* and *specific* arbitrarily in our discussions. This is to say that others may prefer to use different terms for this same purpose, and in the absence of standardized terminology, it is certainly their prerogative to do so. The present chapter is devoted to creative movements designed to relax the entire body (general), and the following chapter is concerned with creative movements for particular muscles or muscle groups (specific).

In considering the creative movement experiences that we are recommending, it appears important to make some general suggestions for their use. The following descriptive list is submitted for this purpose.

    1. Because of their very nature, most creative movement experiences tend to be relaxing. The reason for this is that they are conducted in an informal atmosphere with a minimum amount of formal structuring.

2. Although most children are naturally creative, some will manifest more creativity than others. This means that, depending upon the nature of a particular creative experience, along with the creative level of a child, there is a need to determine the extent of teacher guidance needed in each situation. With practice, most teachers will be able to make a judgment that is in the best interest of the children.
3. A very important aspect in conducting creative movement with children is the teacher's voice. The manner in which a teacher speaks, along with the intonation of certain words, can have a profound influence on children's creative responses. For example, a soft tone of voice tends to make children respond with a slower movement. A sharp or loud tone tends to cause children to respond more vigorously. Even the words can have an influence on children's responses. For instance, words like *hard* and *soft* and *heavy* and *light* are likely to inspire feelings and emotions that will result in varying responses. The important thing to keep uppermost in mind is that there should be a contrasting experience—tensing and letting go. The voice can have a pronounced influence on this experience.
4. Some of the activities are accompanied by prepared stories. Whether or not the teacher wishes to use these stores is an arbitrary matter. A story tends to add more structure to the experience, and this can cause some children to feel more comfortable as they prepare to respond creatively.
5. The format for conducting the various activities is intended only as a general way of organizing the experiences. For this reason, the suggested procedures should be considered as a guide and not necessarily as a prescription to be followed. In other words, individuals should inject their own creative ideas into the procedures for conducting the experiences. The suggested format consists of (a) the name of the activity, (b) suggested teacher input, (c) some possible children's responses, and (d) suggested evaluation procedures.

6. The question of *where* to conduct the activities is important. Some can be conducted while sitting in a chair or on the surface area. Others may require more space. The nature of the activity itself will ordinarily indicate where the activity might best take place. One very important consideration in this regard is that, for those activities that suggest that the child might respond by falling to the surface area, a soft landing surface should be provided for this purpose. This could be a rug or other suitable soft landing surface.

(NOTE: Creative movement responses of children are pretty much an individual matter; that is, each child is likely to respond in the way that the experience means to him personally. Therefore, a creative movement experience can be conducted with a group of children with each child creating his own more or less unique response. At the same time, any of the recommended activities can be presented to a single child. Although the activities can be used with individual children or with groups of children, the indication in the descriptions of the activities is that they are for a group of children).

Activity:

Hard and Soft. A major purpose of this activity is to help the children distinguish between the terms *hard* and *soft*. The opening discussion can be oriented in this direction.

Introduction:

The teacher can ask the children if they know the difference between hard and soft.

Responses:

Children might respond by naming some things that are hard or soft. (If this does not happen, the teacher can guide the discussion with certain questions.)

Teacher:

Is a rock hard?
Can you make a rock soft?
Is the pavement hard?
Can it be made soft?

(The purpose here is to help those children who do not know the difference, or how to explain the difference, to be able to distinguish between hard and soft. All such questions will be governed by the original responses of the children).

Teacher:
We have talked about some of the things that are hard and some that are soft. Now, I wonder if you could do something to make yourself hard?

Responses:
Children respond by creating shapes and positions that depict their bodies as being hard.

Teacher:
Now, can you do something that will make your body feel soft?

Responses:
Children do several things that give them the feeling of a soft body.

Teacher:
All right. Very good. I am going to say the word *hard,* and when you hear it, I want you to make yourself feel hard. After that, I will say the word *soft,* and then you make yourself feel soft. (The teacher calls out the word *hard* and has the children hold their position for three or four seconds before calling out the word *soft.* This can be continued with the teacher using the words harder and hardest and softer and softest. The teacher should take advantage of appropriate intonation of the words *hard* and *soft.*

Evaluation:
A discussion can be developed with questions such as the following:
How did you feel when you were hard?
How did you feel when you were soft?
Did you feel better when you pretended you were hard or when you were soft?
Could you feel the difference?

Activity:
Cold and Hot. In working with children in creative movement, we have found that there are certain conditions that cause children to react more or less "naturally" to specific situations. The activity Cold and Hot is a case in point. When children are asked to respond to *cold* they tend to react with a "tensed

up" body condition. When responding to *hot* they tend to react with a more relaxed state. This is probably because children have had the actual experience of being cold and hot.

Introduction:

The teacher can introduce the discussion by referring to certain climatic or seasonal conditions that will depict cold and hot. Some introductory questions could include the following:

Is a piece of ice hot or cold?

Is the sun hot or cold?

If you have been out on a cold winter day, how did it make you feel?

How does it feel to be outside on a warm summer day?

Can you think of some things that are cold or hot?

(The teacher attempts to guide the discussion in the direction of a person's feelings when the body is cold and/or hot.)

Responses:

Some children are likely to suggest that they shiver when cold and sweat when hot. Others will tell about their experiences with things that are hot and cold.

Teacher:

You have told a lot of things about cold and hot. Now, how would you like to show us how it feels to be cold and how it feels to be hot? When I say the word *cold*, please show us what you would do with your body. When I say the word *hot*, show us what your body would do. (The teacher continues with this procedure as the children create body movements that express hot and cold).

Evaluation:

Did you feel "looser" when you were cold or when you were hot? George, you made your body into a ball when I said "Cold," and when I said "Hot," you flopped over and spread out your arms. Why did you do that? Could you tell us the different feeling you had when you pretended to be cold than when you pretended to be hot?

Activity:

Giant and Dwarf. This activity focuses on what a child will do with his body when he tries to make himself larger and taller contrasted to when he tries to make himself smaller and shorter. It has been observed that, when children try to make themselves tall, more muscle tension occurs. On the contrary, when pretending to be short and small, there is a state of relaxation.

Introduction:

The teacher can take many different approaches in introducing this activity. One would be to comment about the giant and dwarves in the circus. Many children have had the experience of either having been to a circus or having seen one on television.

Responses:

Children are likely to respond by commenting about the size of giants and dwarves and about how they move around — the giant with large steps and the dwarf with small choppy steps. They will also wish to imitate these movements.

Teacher:

I wonder how it would feel to be big and tall like a giant. How do you think it would feel to be small and short like a dwarf? Maybe we should try it. I will say "Giant," then I will say "Dwarf," and you can pretend to be the one that I say. Are you ready? (The teacher alternates calling out "Giant" and "Dwarf" as the children try to make their bodies into the particular designation.)

Evaluation:

You did very well by changing quickly from a giant to a dwarf.

Which was harder, being a giant or a dwarf?

How did your body feel when you tried to be a giant?

How did your body feel when you tried to be a dwarf?

(In the evaluation the discussion might be guided in the direction that everyone should probably be comfortable being what he is and should be satisfied with himself regardless of whether he is large or small).

Activity:

Rain and Snow. This creative experience is like the previous ones; however, it differs because it is likely to be an experience in which most children have not participated on their own. It has been our experience that, when children are asked to imitate rain, they tend to make their bodies tense. When imitating snow, they appear to relax the body. We have speculated that the reason for this is that they generally associate rain as *heavy* and snow as *light*. Some teachers try to guide the discussion in this particular direction.

Introduction:

One good way to introduce this activity is to ask what the difference is between rain and snow.

Responses:

Some typical responses are the following:

Rain is wetter than snow.

Rain comes down harder than snow.

Snow is white; rain does not have color.

It is more fun playing in the snow than it is in the rain.

My mother doesn't care if I play in the snow, but she does not like to have me play in the rain.

Teacher:

You have suggested some very interesting ways in which snow and rain are different. Now, how do you think it would make you feel to pretend you are rain — and then snow.

Responses:

Children express different feelings.

Teacher:

You have told many different ways it could feel to be like rain and snow. Now, let's pretend we are one and then the other. I will say "Rain," and then I will say "Snow." (The teacher alternates calling out "Rain" and "Snow" as the children try to create movements in the form of these two elements).

Evaluation:

Which did you like best — pretending you were rain or pretending you were snow?

How did it feel to be like rain?

How did it feel to be like snow?

When did it feel more restful — when you were rain or when you were snow?

Did you feel heavier when you were rain?

Did you feel lighter when you were snow?

Which one gave you the better feeling?

Creative Movement for General Relaxation

Activity:

Peanut Butter and Milk. This activity is similar to the preceding one because the substances (peanut butter and milk) are concerned with contrasting consistency. Peanut butter is thought of as a thick substance, while milk is thought of as a thin substance.

Introduction:

The discussion can be introduced by raising questions about the two foods as follow:
How many of you drink milk every day?
How many of you have eaten peanut butter?
What is the difference between the two?
What do you think would happen if we tried to pour peanut butter like we pour milk?

Responses:

Children generally respond in terms of the thickness of peanut butter and the thinness of milk. Typical responses are the following:
You don't spread milk like you do peanut butter.
You can't make a sandwich out of milk.
You eat peanut butter, but you drink milk.
You can eat a peanut butter sandwich, and then drink milk.

Teacher:

Those are all good ideas. Now, how do you think it would feel to make your body like peanut butter and then like milk. Let's try it. I will say "Peanut butter," and then I will say "Milk," and you try to change from one to the other.

Evaluation:

How did you feel when you made yourself like peanut butter?
How did you feel when you made yourself like milk?
Was it easier to make yourself like peanut butter or like milk? Which was more fun?

Activity:

Soldiers. In this activity the soldiers are depicted "at attention," and "at ease," or in a tensed and relaxed state. While children are likely to be familiar with the term "attention," such is not likely to be the case with the term "at ease." Therefore, in the discussion the teacher will need to focus on this, and the activity might be introduced as follows:

Introduction:
>We talk a great deal about paying attention.
>What does this mean?

Responses:
>Some typical responses are:
>Listen when someone else is talking.
>Don't talk when you (teacher) are talking.
>Don't make noise.
>Do your work, and don't fool around.

Teacher:
>You know pretty well what it means to "pay attention." Now, in something we are going to do we will use the word *attention*. How many of you have ever seen a solder? (Some children indicate that they have, either in real life or on television or in the movies. The discussion focuses on what a soldier does when standing at attention, and children are asked to demonstrate.)
>
>Mary, can you show us how a soldier would look standing at attention? (Several other children are asked to give their version of this, and the teacher continues.)
>
>You all did very well. Now, soldiers do not stand at attention all of the time. Sometimes they are asked to stand at ease. What do you think is meant by that? (Several children respond in various ways, and again, some are asked to demonstrate.)
>
>All right, let's try both of these, standing at attention and being at ease. I will say first one and then the other.

Evaluation:
>The activity proceeds for a time and is followed by an evaluation using questions such as the following:
>How did it make you feel to stand at attention?
>How did it make you feel to stand at ease?
>Which was easier? Why?

Activity:
>High Wire Walker. This activity is concerned with the tenseness experienced by the high wire walker when performing as compared to the relaxed state when dropping into a net.

Introduction:
>The activity can be introduced by simply asking how many children have seen a circus.

Responses:
   Ordinarily, practically all children will have seen a circus, if not live, then on television.

Teacher:
   What are some of the things you like best about a circus?

Responses:
   Obviously, there will be a large number and variety of responses. It will be very possible that one or more children will name the high wire performance. (If this is not the case, the teacher can guide the discussion to the high wire performance).

Teacher:
   What are some things you would like to say about high wire walkers?

Responses:
   Some typical responses are as follow:
   They are almost at the top.
   They carry a long stick.
   They walk slowly.
   Sometimes they fall in a net.

Teacher:
   (The teacher discusses the responses and continues). Let's try being high wire walkers, and then we can pretend to drop into a net. When I say "Walk," you can pretend you are walking on the high wire. When I say "Drop," you can pretend to drop into the net.

Evaluation:
   What were some of the things you liked about being a high wire walker?
   Did your body feel stiff when you were walking?
   How did it feel when you dropped into the net?
   Was it as much fun dropping into the net as it was walking on the high wire?

Activity:
   The Kite. This activity is concerned with a kite in flight being kept up by the wind. This is compared to when the wind ceases and the kite begins to descend.

Introduction:
In the introductory discussion the teacher poses questions such as the following:
What is a kite?
How many of you have ever had a kite?
Did you ever try to make a kite?
How can you make a kite fly?
What makes a kite stay in the air?
What happens when a kite begins to fall?

Responses:
There will be many various responses, with the teacher attempting to guide the discussion in the direction of the purpose of the activity.

Teacher:
How do you think it would feel to be like a kite up in the air?

Responses:
Children express their feelings, and the teacher encourages them to demonstrate. (Children will perform in many different ways, but the most prevalent way is taking a forward leaning stance with arms outspread to the sides. This tends to cause the muscles of the body to become tense).

Teacher:
You are all very good at being a Kite. Now, let's try being a kite in the air, kept up by the wind, and a kite after the wind stops blowing. When I say "Up," it will mean that you are a kite in the air, and when I say "Down," it will mean that the wind has stopped and the kite comes down.

Evaluation:
How did you feel when you were a kite in the air?
How did you feel when the wind stopped?
What was the difference in your body when you were a kite in the air and when you were a kite when the wind stopped?

Activity:
The Balloon. This activity involves a balloon being blown up to capacity and then the air suddenly being released. A very important feature of this activity is that it helps a child learn about controlled breathing, which is so important to muscular relaxation. This activity provides for rhythm in breathing as

the child inhales deeply, then exhales, and becomes relaxed when the air is released from the balloom.

Introduction:

To begin the discussion the teacher can use questions such as the following:

Did you ever blow up a balloon and then let it go?

What happens if you blow it up too hard?

What happens when you let it go?

(It may be a good idea for the teacher to start the discussion with a real balloon. It can be blown up and then let go with the questions and discussion proceeding from this point).

Responses:

Children will provide many responses verbally, but many times they will immediately try to show what a balloon does when it is let go with air in it.

Teacher:

Good! You are acting like you are a balloon. Now, let's blow up like a balloon, and when I say "Let go," everyone do what a balloon would do when the air comes out.

Evaluation:

Did you feel tight when you took the air in like a balloon?

How did it make you feel when you were holding the air?

How did it make you feel when you let go?

Was it a better feeling to hold the air in or to let it go?

Activity:

Be This, Be That. This activity involves a series of contrasting creative movements. The teacher calls out a tension movement followed by a relaxation movement, with the children responding by creating the movements. The following are some possibilities for such movements, and the creative adult along with the children will be able to think of many others.

Be a Telephone Pole — Be a Feather

Be a Ball Bat — Be a Jump Rope

Be an Icicle — Be a Pillow

Be a Statue — Be a Rubber Band

Be a Broom Handle — Be a Piece of String

Be a Chair — Be a Cushion

Be a Board — Be a Paper Bag

CREATIVE ACTIVE PLAY STORIES

It is very interesting to children when creative movement experiences are presented in the form of a story. Several creative active play stories are provided here that in one way or another involve contrasting tensing-relaxing movements for general relaxation. The stories can be read to children, or depending upon their ability level, children can read the stories themselves.

Creative active play stories are written about some sort of movement experience that children will enjoy performing. It will be noticed that the movement experience depicted in each story is not readily identifiable. The reason for this is that creativity on the part of the child is likely to be diminished if he is given more or less specific directions for performing the activity. In the following selections the story is presented first, and this is followed by a *description* of the activity depicted in the story and a *suggested application*. (The description is given to assist the teacher in guiding the creativity of the child in the performance of the activity).

Franky Frog Jumps

Franky Frog sits.
He is ready.
He jumps.
Sit like Franky.
Jump like Franky.

Description:

The activity depicted in this story is the *frog jump*. A child squats down on feet and hands. He elevates himself off the surface area by springing into the air from both feet and hands and landing on both feet and hands.

Application:

Before the story is read, the children can be engaged in a discussion of frogs and how they move. The discussion can focus on how a frog sits and then suddenly takes a jump. Body tension occurs when the frog (child) is preparing to jump as well as during the jump. There is release of tension at the end of the jump.

Willie Worm

I move like Willie Worm.
I move in front.
I move in back.
I move along.
I will stop quickly.

Description:

The activity in this story is *measuring worm*. A child lies down facing the surface area. He pushes up and places his weight on his hands and the toes. The elbows are straight, and the body is stiff. He brings the feet up close to the hands by walking along while the hands are kept in place. The feet are then kept in place, and he walks along on the hands until the body is extended again. He continues in this manner.

Application:

Discussion starts with how a worm moves. The children are then asked how they might do this. They try to perform the activity under the guidance of the teacher. There is tension of the body as a child prepares to move like a worm. This continues as he moves like Willie Worm. The teacher can give a signal to stop quickly, and at this point there is release of the tensed muscles.

Jumping Jack

I am a Jumping Jack.
I jump way up.
I come way down.
I will jump up and down.

Description:

In the *jumping jack* the child stoops down low in a crouched position. He exerts his energy by jumping up. He tries to land lightly on his feet and then falls to the surface area. (Most activities that require landing should be performed on a soft landing surface such as a carpet or matting.)

Application:

There can be a discussion of how a Jack-in-the-box functions. The children can then try to create the activity. Tension occurs during preparation for the jump and during the jump.

Curly Cat Takes A Walk

Curly Cat is asleep.
Curly Cat opens his eyes.
Curly Cat takes a walk.
He walks with long steps.
He holds his head high.
He walks around.
Try to walk like Curly Cat.
Put your hands on the floor.
Walk all around like Curly Cat.

Description:

In the *cat walk* the child walks along on his hands and feet while trying to maintain an arch in his back.

Application:

The discussion can start by asking how many have a cat as a pet. This can be followed by asking if they have ever watched the cat while it was sleeping and what it did when it awakened. Tension occurs as the child assumes the position for the walk, and it also occurs during the walk. The teacher can suggest that the cat suddenly stop and lie down. It is at this point that the muscles relax.

George Giraffe

There is a tall animal in a far away land.
He has a long neck.
His name is George Giraffe.
You could look like him if you did this.
Place your arms high over your head.
Put your hands together.
Point them to the front.
This will be his neck and head.
Now walk like George Giraffe.
This is how.
Stand on your toes.
Walk with your legs straight.

Description:

In the *giraffe walk* the child stands straight with his arms extended upward. The wrists are bent forward with the fingers pointing straight ahead. The thumbs can be interlocked. The child walks along with his legs stiff.

Application:

The discussion can begin by asking children if they have ever been to a zoo. If some have had this experience, the discussion can focus upon the kinds of animals in the zoo. The teacher can guide the discussion so that attention is directed to a giraffe. If none of the children have been to a zoo, the teacher can ask if they have been to a circus or have seen a circus on television. It is also very useful to begin the discussion with a picture of a giraffe. In assuming the position for the giraffe walk and actually performing the walk, there is a great deal of muscle tension. As in the case of the previous activity (cat walk) the teacher may give a signal for the giraffe to drop to the surface area. This provides for muscular relaxation.

The Jumping Rabbit

I can jump like a rabbit.
I will sit like a rabbit.
I put my hands on the floor.
Now I jump.
My feet come up to my hands.
I hold my hands in front.
I put my hands on the floor.
I jump again and again.
On the last jump I will fall down.

Description:

In the *rabbit jump* the child stoops to a squatting position. The hands are placed on the floor in front. A jump is made with both feet to bring them up close to the hands. The hands are then placed in front again. Several jumps are performed in this manner.

Application:

The teacher can engage the children in any type of discussion that involves rabbits and their habits. In this discussion, consideration can be given regarding how rabbits move. There is tension in the preparation for the jump and the jump itself. There is relaxation when the rabbit falls over on the last jump.

The Growing Flowers

Flowers grow.
First they are seeds.
Be a seed.
Grow like a flower.
Grow and Grow.
Keep growing.
Grow tall.
Now you are a flower.
Now, wilt like a flower.

Description:

In this activity, a child acts out the growth of a flower; the starting position is one in which the child squats down low as close to the surface area as possible. He then stretches (grows) as tall as he can.

Application:

A real flower or a picture of a flower can be used in the discussion about flowers. The discussion can take into account the various kinds of flowers, what they need to make them grow, and how they grow. Tension occurs during the growing period, and there is relaxation when the flower wilts.

Falling Leaves

Trees stand tall and straight.
Stand tall and straight like a tree.
Trees have leaves.
Leaves fall.
They fall from the trees.
They fall to the ground.
Fall like leaves.
Down, down, down.
Down to the ground.
Quiet leaves.
Rest like leaves.

Description:

This is a creative experience in which the child dramatizes leaves falling from a tree. The child stands straight and stiff like a tree and then creates movements that depict falling leaves.

Application:

This activity can be introduced with any discussion about trees and their leaves. Tension occurs during the time the child stands stiff like a tree, and relaxation takes place as the child releases from this position and acts out the falling of leaves.

Mr. Snowman and Mr. Sun

See Mr. Snowman.
Mr. Snowman is packed hard with snow.
See Mr. Sun.
Mr. Sun is warm.
Mr. Snowman sees Mr. Sun.
Mr. Snowman is going.
Going, going, going.
Mr. Snowman is gone.
Be Mr. Snowman.

Description:

This creative activity is one in which a child dramatizes a melting snowman. In doing this, the child will create his idea of a snowman and what happens when the snowman melts.

Application:

There are many ways to introduce this activity. One of the most effective ways is to discuss the building of a snowman and how long it will last. Reasons why a snowman melts can be discussed. The child's body is tense as he becomes a snowman of hard packed snow. Relaxation occurs when he melts by being in the sun.

All of the creative movement experiences presented in this chapter have been tested under various circumstances, and they have met with a great deal of success when used with children. They have been very useful as a means of helping to reduce stress in children in a way that is enjoyable for them. In addition, the use of these kinds of activities can play a large part in helping children understand about the stress phenomenon, particularly as it pertains to tension and relaxation.

With reference to the creative active play stories, it is entirely possible that some of you will want to try to develop some of your own stories, and we heartily recommend that you try your hand at it. Should this be the case the following guidelines are submitted for consideration:

1. In general, the *new* word load should be kept relatively low.
2. When new words are used, there should be as much repetition of these words as possible and appropriate.
3. Sentence length and lack of complex sentences should be considered in keeping the level of difficulty of material within the ability level of children.
4. Consideration should also be given to the reading values and literary merits of a story. Using a character or characters in a story setting help to develop interest.
5. The activity to be used in the creative active play story should *not* be readily identifiable. When children identify an activity early in the story, there can be resulting minimum attention on their part to get the necessary details to engage in the creative active play experience. Of course, the teacher plays a very important part in guiding the creative experience.

Chapter 7

CREATIVE MOVEMENTS FOR SPECIFIC RELAXATION

AT the outset of this chapter it might be useful to repeat again our meaning of the terms *general* and *specific* relaxation. General relaxation is concerned with the entire body, while specific relaxation pertains to specific muscles or body parts. An interesting feature of specific relaxation is that it not only relaxes specific body parts, but at the same time, it makes it easier for the child to learn about the tensing-releasing phenomenon. It is easier to recognize this when just certain specific muscles are involved.

Most of the procedures recommended in the preceding chapter apply in the present chapter; however, the creative movements in this chapter will be organized under headings of specific muscle groups. These are the same classifications used in chapter 4, that is, (1) muscles of the head, face, tongue, and neck; (2) muscles of the trunk; (3) muscles of the upper extremities; and (4) muscles of the lower extremities. (It should be recalled that a number of muscles situated in the trunk may be grouped with the muscles of the upper extremities, their function being to attach the upper limbs to the trunk and move the shoulders and arms; this means that there can be some overlapping from one muscle group to another.) There are a number of creative active play stories in this chapter, and they will be organized under the appropriate headings in the same manner, rather than as a separate classification as in chapter 6. The reader should notice that some of the activities in this chapter involve a certain degree of structuring. This means that the children should still be free to explore various ways of performing an activity. At the same time, the teacher should provide enough guidance in the creative response to direct the performance of an activity in a manner in which the objective of the activity will be reached.

MUSCLES OF THE HEAD, FACE, TONGUE, AND NECK

(Children particularly enjoy activities in this muscle group because it gives them an opportunity to make "funny faces" legitimately.)

Activity:

Big Eye. In this activity the eyes are opened as wide as possible for a period of about four to six seconds. Also, the person can look to the right, left, above, and below.

Introduction:

The teacher can name the activity and ask the children what they think it means.

Responses:

Some children will immediately respond by opening their eyes very wide.

Teacher:

When I say "Big Eye," try to open your eyes wide and hold it until I say "Little Eye."

Evaluation:

How did it feel to have a big eye? Did it feel different to have a little eye?

Activity:

The Sneeze. The muscles are contracted on either side of the nose as in sneezing. The skin should be wrinkled upward over the nose as hard as possible.

Introduction:

The activity can be introduced by discussion of how one looks when sneezing. There can also be a discussion of what causes one to sneeze.

Responses:

The children consider this to be a very funny activity, and they will respond in a variety of ways. Some of them will immediately try to do a forced sneeze.

Teacher:
   I want you to show how you would look when you are getting ready to sneeze. When I say "Ready," everyone pretend to get ready to sneeze. When I say "Sneeze" everyone pretend to sneeze.

Evaluation:
   Did your face feel tight when you were getting ready to sneeze? How did your face feel after you pretended to sneeze?

Activity:
   Rabbit Nose. This activity involves dilating and flaring out the nostrils.

Introduction:
   The discussion can be introduced by considering how rabbits move, the color of their fur, and other features.

Responses:
   Some children will have either had a pet rabbit or will have seen one in a pet store. They are very willing to tell many things that they know about them because rabbits are a favorite with children.

Teacher:
   (If none of the children respond about the quick movements that a rabbit makes with its nose, the teacher can point the discussion in this direction.) Have you ever noticed how rabbits make their noses move out and in? I wonder why they do this? Maybe we could pretend to be rabbits and make this movement with our noses. When I say "Out," pretend to make a rabbit nose. When I say "Stop," let your nose change back to the way it was before.

Evaluation:
   Did your nose feel tight when you made a rabbit nose? How did it feel when you let your nose change back?

Activity:
   The Frown. There are many ways to perform this activity, which include (1) stretching the left corner of the mouth up and out, (3) stretching the right corner of the mouth down and out, (4) stretching the left corner of the mouth down and out, and (5) stretching the lower lip down hard while trying to keep the lip flat.

Introduction:
> A discussion can begin about smiling and frowning, with consideration of how they are alike and different, why people smile and frown, and what it means to keep a "straight" face. Also the teacher can mention the different kinds of frowns suggested above.

Responses:
> While children will respond verbally, more often than not, they will immediately respond by frowning and smiling.

Teacher:
> Let's play a game in which we will use different kinds of frowns. Remember the different kinds of frowns we talked about. When I say "Frown," make any kind of frown you please, and hold it until I say "Straight." This means that you should quickly change from the frown to a straight face.

Evaluation:
> Was your face stiff when you frowned? Did your face feel loose when you changed from a frown to a straight face? What do you think happened?

Activity:
> The Hard Whistle. The movement in this activity is with the lips, as in whistling, but it is done by tensing the lips vigorously.

Introduction:
> The discussion can begin by asking how many can whistle. This can be followed by a consideration of what causes the whistling sound.

Responses:
> The responses can be noisy because those children who can do so are likely to begin immediately to whistle.

Teacher:
> Did you notice the shape of your mouth and lips? They formed a circle. Now, let's try what we will call the hard whistle. What does that suggest to you?

Responses:
> Children give various comments on the position of the lips in the hard whistle.

Teacher:
   Let's try the hard whistle, when I say "Whistle." When I say "Stop," let your lips go back to the regular position.

Evaluation:
   What kind of feeling did you have on your mouth and lips when you did the hard whistle? Did your lips feel tight? How did they feel when you stopped?

Activity:
   The Silent Yell. In this activity the mouth is opened wide in any direction. This position is held until the release.

Introduction:
   The teacher can start the discussion by mentioning that children call out to each other when they are playing outside. The question can be raised of what these calls are named.

Responses:
   Children give these calls different names, and someone is likely to say they are yelling. If not, this can be mentioned by the teacher.

Teacher:
   (The discussion can be continued by considering why people yell, as well as the sounds made by yelling. Finally, the discussion can be directed to the shape of the face when yelling.) Now, let's try doing what we will call the silent yell. When I say "Yell," act like you are yelling, but do not make a sound. When I say "Stop," let your face return to the regular position.

Evaluation:
   Did your face feel stiff when you acted like you were yelling? How did it feel when you stopped?

MUSCLES OF THE TRUNK

(The activities in this classification are presented in the form of creative active play stories, and the same format is applied as in chapter 6.)

Casper Camel

Casper Camel lives in the zoo.
He has a hump on his back.

He has a hump on his back.
Could you look like Casper Camel?
You will need a hump.
Try it this way.
Bend forward.
Put your arms behind your back.
Hold them together.
That will be a hump.
That will look like Casper Camel.
Take a step.
Lift your head.
Take a step.
Lift your head.
Move like Casper Camel.

Description:

The activity depicted in this story is the *camel walk*. The child stands straight. The hands are placed behind the back and folded. Next, the child bends forward at the waist and tries to raise the arms in the back. The child walks along swinging from side to side.

Application:

Before the story is read to the children a discussion can focus on camels and how they walk. It might be a good idea to show a picture of a camel. Tension of the muscles of the trunk occurs when the child is preparing for the camel walk and when the movement is actually executed. After the child performs the activity for a short time, the teacher can give a call for the camel to fall, and this action releases tension.

The Clowns Do a Stunt

Have you ever seen clowns at a circus?
Sometimes they do funny things.
Once I saw two clowns do a stunt together.
This is what they did.
They sat back to back.
Their feet were flat on the floor.
Their feet were close to their bodies.
They locked their arms together.
They pushed their backs together.

Creative Movement for Specific Relaxation

They pushed hard.
As they pushed, they began to rise.
At last they were standing.
They sat down and did the stunt again.
Could you do this stunt with a friend?

Description:

This story is written about the stunt called *back-to-back get up*. It requires two children of about equal size. Success in performing the stunt depends upon each child pushing hard against the other to rise to the standing position.

Application:

A discussion can be introduced about clowns and the many kinds of things they do to make people laugh. The story can then be read to the children, and they can experiment with the stunt. A great deal of tension occurs when they are rising to the standing position, and it is relieved when they reach this position.

Row Your Boat

You will need a partner to play "Row Your Boat."
Sit down facing your partner.
Put your feet together.
Reach out, and take hold of hands.
Now you are in a boat.
Pull each other back and forth to row your boat.
Sing as you row.
Row to the beat of the music.

> Row, row, row your boat,
>   pulling to and fro.
> Happily, happily, happily, happily,
>   singing as you row.
> Row, row, row your boat,
>   up the stream you go.
> Happily, happily, happily, happily,
>   singing as you row.

Description:

Two children of nearly the same size sit opposite each other and join hands. As the music is played or as they sing, they pull vigorously back and forth.

Application:

The introductory discussion can focus on boats and on what one has to do when rowing a boat. The story can be introduced, and the children can practice the song before engaging in the activity. There is tension in the trunk muscles when rowing the boat. It is released when the song is ended or when the musical accompaniment stops. The muscles of the upper and lower extremities are also involved in this activity.

Circus Elephant

I saw the circus.
I saw many animals.
I saw an elephant.
He was big.
He had big legs.
He had a trunk.
He swings his trunk.
I will walk like the elephant.

Description:

This is the story about the stunt called the *elephant walk*. The child bends forward at the waist with knees straight. The arms are held straight down in front with the hands clasped. The child walks along slowly without bending the knees, swinging the arms from side to side.

Application:

The discussion can begin with circus elephants and how they move and what they do in the circus. There is tension in the muscles of the trunk as the child walks along with legs and arms stiff. To release the tension a signal can be given by the teacher for the elephant to fall down.

MUSCLES OF THE UPPER EXTREMITIES

Activity:

The Squeezer. This activity involves squeezing an imaginary object. It is simply concerned with making a tightly clenched fist and then releasing to an open hand.

Introduction:

The discussion can start with the teacher asking what is meant by the word squeeze, how the squeeze is accomplished, and under what conditions it is done.

Responses:

Children will give all sorts of responses, some of which include the following:

You squeeze lemons.

You squeeze tight on a bat when hitting a ball.

I like to squeeze a toothpaste tube. I once squeezed a cherry, and the seed popped out.

Teacher:

There are certainly many things to squeeze and ways to squeeze them. The kind of squeeze I am thinking about is one in which you would use your whole hand to squeeze something, let's say like a small rubber ball. Let's try it. When I say "Squeeze," everyone pretend to squeeze something in your hand. You can use both hands to pretend you have something in each hand. I will then say "Open," and you can stop squeezing and let your hand come open.

Evaluation:

Did your hands get tired when you squeezed hard? How did it feel when I said "Open"?

Activity:

The Rubber Band. One way to be like a rubber band is to clasp the hands tightly in front of the chest with the elbows pointing out to the sides. The idea of the rubber band is shown when the performer tries as hard as possible to pull the hands apart.

Introduction:

A discussion can focus on rubber bands and their uses. Different sized rubber bands can be presented and stretched to various lengths. (This is exciting for the children because they wonder if the rubber band is going to break.)

Responses:

Children will enter eagerly into a discussion about rubber bands because practically all of them will have had some sort of experience with them.

Teacher:

I wonder how it would feel to be a rubber band and stretch like one? Let's try some movements that would make us be like a rubber band.

Responses:

Children do a large variety of movements depicting a rubber band.

Teacher:

I noticed that some of you held your hands together like your arms were a rubber band. (If this does not happen, it could possibly be suggested by the teacher.) Let's try to stretch the rubber band until it breaks. When I say "Start," try to stretch very hard like a rubber band. When I say "Snap," pretend that the rubber band breaks.

Evaluation:

Did your arms get tired quickly when you were stretching them like a rubber band? Did your hands and arms feel tight? How did it feel when I said "Snap"?

Activity:

The Weight Lifter. This activity is concerned with lifting an imaginary weight, while at the same time straining, as if actually lifting a heavy weight. The kind of lift we are thinking of here is known as the "curl." The lifter stands upright. The weight is on the floor in front. The performer bends at the knees, stoops, and picks up the weight with both hands, "curling" it to the chest.

Introduction:

The discussion can be introduced by asking what is meant by the term *weight lifter*.

Responses:

Since weight lifting has become a popular event, many children will have seen the activity on television. They are very interested in the strength it takes to lift the heavy weights.

Teacher:

(The discussion is focused on various ways to lift weights with emphasis on the curl.) What do you think we mean when we say that one way of lifting a weight is the curl?

Responses:
  Some children will know immediately, and the discussion can be directed to why it is called the curl (weight is curled by the arms up to the chest).

Teacher:
  Let's see if we can be weight lifters and try the curl. When I say "Curl," pretend you are lifting a heavy weight. When I say "Stop," pretend to drop the weight.

Evaluation:
  Did your arms feel tight when you were lifting the weight? Did your arms get a tired feeling? How did it feel when the weight was dropped?

The last three activities in this classification are presented in the form of creative active play stories.

Tick, Tock

Listen to the clock.
It says, "Tick, tock" as it keeps the time.
Would you like to play you are a clock?
This is the way.
Stand up.
Keep your arms straight.
Now keep time with the clock by moving your arms.
Ready.
Move your arms like a clock.
Keep your arms stiff and straight.
Here are some words to say to the "tick, tock" of the clock.

  Tick, tock, tick, tock
  Be bright and gay.
  It's time to start another day.
  Tick, tock, tick, tock,
  Tick, tock, tick, tock,
  Oh! Oh! Let's stop the clock.

Description:
  In this activity the children pretend they are clocks. They use their arms as the hands of the clock. They move the arms as they say the verse.

Application:

A discussion can begin about clocks and about why we need them. Children are asked to pretend to be a clock, and attention is focused on the hands of a clock. The arms are held very rigid as they move like the hands of a clock. When the clock stops, the arms are dropped and, thus, relaxed.

Push the Wheelbarrow

Have you ever seen a wheelbarrow go?
You can play you are a wheelbarrow.
You will need a friend to play with you.
You can be the wheelbarrow.
You get down on your hands and knees.
Your hands will be the wheel.
You walk along on your hands.
Your friend steers the wheelbarrow.
Whoops! The wheelbarrow breaks down.
Now your friend can be the wheelbarrow.
You can steer the wheelbarrow.
Oh! Oh! The wheelbarrow breaks down again.

Description:

The stunt depicted in the story is *the wheelbarrow*. A child has a partner of about equal size and strength. One child of the couple assumes a position with the hands on the floor with elbows straight and feet extended behind. The other child carries the feet of the first child, who keeps his knees straight. The child becomes a wheelbarrow by walking on his hands. Children change positions so that each can be the wheelbarrow.

Application:

The discussion can begin about wheelbarrows, including what they are are, how they run, and what can be done with them. Children are asked to think of ways that they could be a wheelbarrow. When the activity is performed, the child who is the wheelbarrow experiences a great deal of tension in the arms. There is relaxation when the wheelbarrow breaks down.

Creative Movement for Specific Relaxation

Airplanes Go

I look up.
I hold my arms out.
I am an airplane.
My arms are the wings.
They are stiff.
I go round and round.
I stop.

Description:

In this activity the performer pretends to be an airplane, using the arms as the wings of the plane.

Application:

Any discussion about airplanes is a lively one, and children like to pretend to be an airplane. Emphasis is placed on the importance of the wings and that they must be very strong. This tends to prompt the performer to hold the arms out very straight and stiff. Relaxation occurs when the airplane stops.

MUSCLES OF THE LOWER EXTREMITIES

Activity:

Ankle Snap. In this activity the ankle is flexed (bent) very hard toward the body in order to stretch the muscles at the back of the legs from the knee down. This position is held for a short period, and then the foot is extended outward for a short period. Finally, the position is released, relaxing the muscles. Each ankle can be flexed and extended separately.

Introduction:

The discussion can center around the various extremities of the body with reference to how the different kinds of joints can bend (be flexed). The activity can be named, and the teacher can ask what they think is meant by it.

Responses:

The kind of introduction mentioned above will likely result in many kinds of responses indicating experiences children have had with various body joints.

Teacher:

(The teacher takes into account the different responses and then attempts to direct these to the activity.) You have suggested many things that can be done with the ankles. Could you show us some of these things.

Responses:
Children react with different ankle movements. If the teacher notices a movement similar to the ankle snap, this is pointed out.

Teacher:
Let's play the ankle snap game. When I say "Stretch in," try to do this, and when I say "Stretch out," try to do that. When I say "Snap," quickly stop stretching the ankle.

Evaluation:
Did you stretch as hard as you could? How did it feel? Did you feel a change when I said "Snap"? How did that feel?

Activity:
Kick Up. This activity is best accomplished from a sitting position in a chair or the edge of a desk or table. The sitting position should be such that the edge is under the knee. One leg is extended and held for a short period. The extended leg should be very stiff. After the short period, the leg is allowed to bend back to the original position. Each leg can be extended separately.

Introduction:
The discussion can begin by asking about kicking as a movement. Particular reference can be made to its use as a skill in certain kinds of activities.

Responses:
Children are likely to mention games in which the skill of kicking is used such as football, soccer, and the popular game of kickball played in many schools.

Teacher:
(After the discussion about kicking in general, the question is raised about kicking from a sitting position.)

Responses:
This will, of course, evoke many different reactions because children will not be likely to think of kicking being used in this manner.

Teacher:
There is an activity called the kick up. What does this mean to you? Let's try it. When I say "Kick up," will you please do so,

and hold it until I say "Down."

Evaluation:

How did it feel to kick up? Did your leg feel stiff? Did your leg get tired when you held it up? How did it feel when I said "Down"?

The last two activities in this classification are presented in the form of creative active play stories.

Sidney Seal

Did you ever hear of a sea lion?
Sometimes he is called a seal.
He lives in the sea.
Sometimes he lives in the zoo.
There is one in the zoo called Sidney Seal.
He likes to swim.
He can also walk on land.
Would you like to try to walk like Sidney Seal?
Try it this way.
Put your hands on the floor.
Put your feet back.
Put your weight on your hands and on top of your toes.
Now walk on your hands and drag your legs.
Sidney Seal gets tired and falls down.

Description:

The activity that is well depicted in the story is the *seal walk*. The child moves along on the hands and drags the legs behind. The legs are held very rigid.

Application:

The discussion can focus on seals, especially their habits and the different ways they can move. Many children will have seen them on television, if not in real life at the circus. One of the things that they tend to remember about seals is the way they can balance objects and the sounds they make. Although this activity places some tension on the arms, there is also a great deal of muscular rigidity of the legs. The emphasis is placed on keeping the legs as stiff as possible as the seal walks. This tension is released when the seal falls down.

Oliver Ostrich

There is a big bird at the zoo.
His name is Oliver Ostrich.
How could you look like Oliver Ostrich?
I wonder if you could walk like Oliver Ostrich.
Do you want to try?
First, bend forward.
Keep your knees straight.
Hold your ankles.
Now walk like Oliver Ostrich.
Oliver Ostrich is tired.
He sits down.

Description:

In the *ostrich walk* the performer bends at the waist and grasps the ankles. Keeping the legs stiff and straight, he walks along in this position. If the performer cannot bend far enough to grasp the ankles, he bends as far as he can and grasps the legs at any point above the ankles.

Application:

It is probably a good idea to begin the discussion by showing pictures of an ostrich. The reason for this is that it may be unlikely that many children will have seen one. Main emphasis should be placed on the size of the bird and how it moves in comparison to other birds. In the *ostrich walk* much tension is placed on the muscles in the back of the legs. This tension is released when the ostrich sits down.

In summary, perhaps it should be reiterated that all of the activities presented have been field tested with many children. They have met with a great deal of success as a means of relieving tension and, thus, of helping to reduce stress.

The activities for creative relaxation that have been suggested in this book should be considered as representative examples of an almost unlimited number of possibilities. These activities have numerous possible variations that will be immediately noticed by the discerning reader. Therefore, it is heartily recommended that these activities be used as a point of departure for the development of other movements for creative relaxation.

INDEX

A

ACTH, 11
adrenalin, 11
adrenals, 11
Aikman, Ann, 72
anxiety, 6-7, 49-52
    meaning of, 6-7
    school, 49-52
    test, 50-52
APAV technique, 81-83

B

basal metabolic rate, 56
Bednarova, N., 75
Benson, Herbert, 62
Bird, John, 77
Brooke, J. D., 10
Brown, Barbara B., 62

C

competition, 53-54
cooperation, 53
corticoids, 11
Cratty, Bryant J., 69, 76
Creative Active Play Stories, 100
creative movement, 80-122
    approaches to the use of, 83-86
    for general relaxation, 88-106
        Be This, Be That, 99
        Cold and Hot, 91-92
        Curly Cat Takes a Walk, 102
        Falling Leaves, 104
        Franky Frog Jumps, 100
        George Giraffe, 102-103
        Giant and Dwarf, 92-93
        Growing Flowers, 104
        Hard and Soft, 90-91
        High Wire Walker, 96-97
        Jumping Jack, 101
        Mr. Snowman and Mr. Sun, 105
        Peanut Butter and Milk, 95
        Rain and Snow, 93-95
        Soldiers, 95-96
        The Balloon, 98-99
        The Jumping Rabbit, 103
        The Kite, 97-98
        Willie Worm, 101
    for specific relaxation, 107-122
        Airplanes Go, 119
        Ankle Snap, 119
        Big Eye, 108
        Casper Camel, 111-112
        Circus Elephant, 114
        Kick Up, 120-121
        Oliver Ostrich, 122
        Push the Wheelbarrow, 118
        Row Your Boat, 113
        Sidney Seal, 121
        The Clowns do a Stunt, 112-113
        The Frown, 109-110
        The Hard Whistle, 110-111
        The Rubber Band, 115-116
        The Silent Yell, 111-112
        The Sneeze, 108-109
        The Squeezer, 114-115
        The Weight Lifter, 116-117
        Tick Tock, 117-118

some principes of learning applied to, 86-87
creativity, 80-81
Culligan, Matthew J., 19

E

emotional arousals and reactions, 27-29
emotional behavior of children, 36-39
emotional development, 25-31, 33-36, 39-40
    guidelines for children, 33-35
    opportunities for in-home and school environment, 35-36
    evaluating influence of the environment on, 39-40
    factors concerning, 25-31
emotional needs of children, 31-33
emotionality, 25-27
    childhood characteristics of, 26-27
    factors that influence, 29-31
emotionally healthy person, 40-41
emotions, 6, 24-42
    childhood, 24-42
    meaning of, 6
endocrine, 11

G

Gal, Reuven, 73
general adaptation syndrome, 11-12
Goldstein, A. P., 70

H

Hill, K. T., 50
Holland, Margaret, 43
Hopkins, Dave, 77
hormone, 11
Horney, Karen, 53
Humphrey, James H., 7, 46, 52, 54, 64, 81
Humphrey, Joy N., 7, 46, 52, 54, 64, 81
hypothalamus, 11

I

isometric, 73
isotonic, 73

J

Jacobson, Edmund, 64
Jencks, Beata, 72
Johnson, Carol A., 48
Johnson, D. I., 76

K

Kanfer, F., 70
Kaplan, C., 52
Keat, D. B., 76
Kirkland, M. C., 51
Krampf, Harry, 77

L

Lazarus, Richard S., 73
Luria, A. R., 69

M

Mason, John W., 12
McBrien, Robert J., 71, 76
McQuade, Walter, 72

P

Passer, Michael, 53
Pellitier, Kenneth R., 47
physical activity and exercise, 71-72
    importance of in coping with stress, 72
pituitary, 11

R

recreation, 63-64
refreshment, 63
relaxation, 62-79
    and stress reduction, 62-79
    creative, 78-79
    creative movements for, 88-122
    differential, 88
    for teachers in the classroom, 71
    general, 88-106
    meaning of, 62-63
    mental practice and imagery in, 69-71

Index

of various muscles, 66-69
progressive, 64-69
response, 62
specific, 107-122
using with children, 75-78
Robin, A., 70
Robinson, H. B., 37
Roedell, W., 37
Rutter, Michael, 46

S

Sarasen, S. B., 50
Scanlan, Tara K., 53
Schneider, M., 70
Schuessler, Raymond, 19
Sedlacek, Keith, 19
Selye, Hans, 5, 11, 12, 18
sex differences in early school success, 54-58
Slaby, R. G., 37
Spielberger, C. D., 76
Steinhaus, Arthur, 63
stress, 3-23, 43-61
    and the child in the educational process, 49-50
    desirable, 18-19
    emotional, 17-18
    factors that induce in children, 43-61
        home conditions, 46-49
        school anxieties, 49-52
        self concerns, 44-46
        teacher behaviors, 52-54
    helping children understand the concept of, 19-23
    meaning of, 4-5
    physical, 16-17
    reactions to, 13-15
        behavioral, 14-15
        physiological, 13-14
    some principles to apply in dealing with, 58-61
    teachers' concepts of, 7-10
    terminology, 4
    theories of, 10-13

T

tension, 5-6
thymus, 11

V

Viscott, David, 7

W

Walker, C. Eugene, 7, 70
Whiting, H. T. A., 10, 69

155.412 H885r　　　　　　c.1
Humphrey, James Harr
Reducing stress in children th　180101 000

3 9318 00002345 8
ST. FRANCIS COLLEGE LIBRARY

The Library
University of Saint Francis
2701 Spring Street
Fort Wayne, Indiana 46808

WITHDRAWN